PRAISE FOR
LOVE 'EM OR LOSE 'EM

"There is no issue with greater urgency, or with more far-reaching consequences, than the issue of retention. The authors have done corporate America a great favor by focusing a laser beam on the subject. They have skillfully blended wit, humor, charm, research and common sense to grab the reader's attention and inspire action. Their book provides easy to implement answers for everything you always wanted to know about retention, but were afraid to ask."

—DEEPAK (DICK) SETHI, DIRECTOR, EXECUTIVE & LEADERSHIP DEVELOPMENT, THE THOMSON CORPORATION

"*Love 'Em or Lose 'Em* offers busy managers a fresh viewpoint that clearly links business success to retention of talent. Realistic and practical, it focuses on the #1 business issue of the 21st Century!"

—RICHARD J. LEIDER, FOUNDER, THE INVENTURE GROUP, AUTHOR OF *THE POWER OF PURPOSE* AND COAUTHOR OF *REPACKING YOUR BAGS*

"Kaye and Jordan-Evans have provided a very useful road-map for leaders who are trying to manage the retention issue. This book belongs in every manager's resource library."

—RICHARD BECKHARD, PROFESSOR OF MANAGEMENT (RETIRED), SLOAN SCHOOL OF MANAGEMENT, MIT

"The common thread in the Internet and entertainment industries, and other technology industries as well, is a manic obsession with hiring and retaining talented employees. Although Kaye and Jordan-Evans won't hire them for you, they will give you and your managers a workable set of actions and attitudes to retain your rock stars. Kaye and Jordan-Evans demonstrate that retention, like hiring, is totally in your control."

—DAVID CODIGA, SENIOR VICE PRESIDENT, GEOCITIES, AND FORMER EXECUTIVE VICE PRESIDENT, UNIVERSAL STUDIOS

"A down-to-earth book for making retention happen. Here is a no-nonsense, common-sense, practical, 'how-to' handbook for keeping your 'seeds' for the future motivated, challenged, and rewarded. Written for every level of management, the authors present valid research findings on what you need to do to retain your valued employees."

—Frederic M. Hudson, Ph.D., President,
the Hudson Institute of Santa Barbara

"A fervently passionate book about a deeply serious subject. With knowing wit and practical intelligence, Kaye and Jordan-Evans present us with elegant solutions and engaging examples of how to deal with the most vexing problem organizations now confront— attracting and retaining the very best talent. Based on a solid foundation of broad-based research, *Love 'Em or Lose 'Em* will fill you with a burning sense of urgency, a renewed faith in your own leadership abilities, and a feeling of delight that you took the time to read and use it."

—Jim Kouzes, coauthor of *The Leadership Challenge* and
Encouraging the Heart, and Chairman, Tom Peters Group/Learning Systems

"At a time when many managers struggle to access the potential of Generation X employees and others who are 'different' in some fashion, Kaye and Jordan-Evans offer a user-friendly, practical guide that reflects the realities of diversity. *Love 'Em or Lose 'Em* challenges managers not to simply accept the loss of employees, but rather to embrace responsibility for the critical tasks of developing and retaining talent."

—Dr. Roosevelt Thomas, Jr.,
author of *Redefining Diversity* and *Beyond Race and Gender*

"Kaye and Jordan-Evans have given leaders of organizations an action plan for how 'not to lose' those knowledge assets of a company. If you have time for only one book, this is the one to read!"

— Jane Michel, Senior Consultant,
Quality & Performance Improvement, Chevron Corporation

LOVE 'EM
— OR —
LOSE 'EM

Also by Beverly Kaye

Designing Career Development Systems
(with Zandy B. Leibowitz and Caela Farren)

Up Is Not the Only Way: A Guide to Developing Workforce Talent

LOVE 'EM
— OR —
LOSE 'EM

GETTING GOOD PEOPLE TO STAY

BEVERLY KAYE AND SHARON JORDAN–EVANS

Berrett-Koehler Publishers, Inc.
San Francisco

Berrett-Koehler Publishers, Inc.
450 Sansome Street, Suite 1200
San Francisco, CA 94111-3320
Tel: (415) 288-0260   Fax: (415)362-2512   www.bkconnection.com

ORDERING INFORMATION

Quantity sales. Special discounts are available on quantity purchases by corporations, associations, and others. For details, contact the "Special Sales Department" at the Berrett-Koehler address above.

Individual sales. Berrett-Koehler publications are available through most bookstores. They can also be ordered direct from Berrett-Koehler: Tel: (800) 929-2929; Fax: (802) 864-7626; www.bkconnection.com

Orders for college textbook/course adoption use. Please contact Berrett-Koehler: Tel: (800) 929-2929; Fax: (802) 864-7626.

Orders by U.S. trade bookstores and wholesalers. Please contact Publishers Group West, 1700 Fourth Street, Berkeley, CA 94710. Tel: (510) 528-1444; Fax (510) 528-3444.

Printed in the United States of America

Library of Congress Cataloging-in-Publication Data
Kaye, Beverly L.
   Love 'em or lose 'em : getting good people to stay / Beverly Kaye and
Sharon Jordan-Evans.
      p. cm.
   Includes bibliographical references and index.
   ISBN 1-57675-073-6 (alk. paper)
   1. Employee retention.   2. Labor turnover.   I. Jordan-Evans,
Sharon, 1946–   II. Title.
HF5549.5.R58K39   1999
658.3'14—dc21   99-38557
                                                              CIP

First Edition
05 04 03 02 01 00 99   10 9 8 7 6 5 4 3 2

Interior design and production: Joan Keyes, Dovetail Publishing Services
Cover design and interior art: Tracy Mitchell

To our families, who have always shown us the "Love 'Em" part . . .

—Bev & Sharon

Table of Contents

 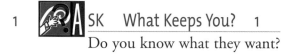

Preface

We believe that managers and supervisors have the most critical role to play in winning the race for talent. We also believe that many managers and supervisors are abdicating this role because they feel that the key retention strategies are out of their hands. Many think it is largely about money, perks and benefits—areas over which they have no control. We know that is not the case.

So we decided to write a book *to* and *for* managers. Busy managers. People who are doing more with less and find that time is their most prized commodity. It had to be brief and to the point. Yet it had to make a strong argument, backed up with data, and full of easy-to-do recommendations.

And so we began our research. We spent about two years collecting focus group information in companies of all sizes and with employees of all levels. We conducted the same research in diverse groups of friends and professional colleagues. The key question we asked led us to the first chapter in this book. We asked: "What kept you?" We compared and contrasted the data with a key factor list until we were convinced that most of the keys to retaining talented employees are in the control of the manager. We also worked the Internet. We collected information from newspapers, journals, books and stories from folks we met along the way. All of the data was then divided into our 26 alphabetical categories. The names of those categories (chapter titles) shifted until we found ones that held all of the data.

We also used a continuing series of focus groups—H.R. professionals, managers and supervisors, pals, relatives, clients, spouses and airplane seatmates—to test all of our ideas. We debated. We revised. We influenced. We agreed. And the final set of 26 chapters/strategies that appear in this book surfaced.

To make the book as practical and useful as possible, we include these elements in each chapter:

1.   **To Do Lists.** The what and why of the race to retain talent are mostly known; we never get enough of the how-tos.

2.   **Alas Stories.** We've included our own collection of "the-fish-that-got-away" stories. These "alas" tales are all true and draw on our combined 40 years of experience in a great variety of organizations nationally and internationally.

3.   **One Employee's Exit.** A.J., our ubiquitous ex-employee (and yes, we mean for you not to know A.J.'s gender, age or job title) appears in each chapter to let you know how that particular strategy (or lack of it) influenced one individual's decision to leave.

4.   **Company Examples.** We've included examples from retention work that we have done with our own clients. We also pulled stories and examples from the literature (newspapers, journals, popular magazines).

5.   **Go To Icons.** Most chapters include at least one recommendation of another chapter that amplifies or augments a key point. This enables you to skip around to find the ideas that are most relevant and important to you.

The Manager's Role

Much of the advice and content points in the 26 chapters will not be new to you. But their use as retention strategies might be. We are passionate about the fact that you *do* make a difference, and we try not to mince words.

We Want You To...

✓   Use this as your guidebook.
✓   Return to it again and again.
✓   Dog-ear the page corners.

✓ Use a highlighter on what matters most.
✓ Put a bookmark in certain chapters and leave the book on your *own* manager's desk!
✓ Personally commit to implementing just one chapter!

Our bottom line is that *Love 'Em or Lose 'Em* will make your life easier. It will help you in a real-time, day-to-day way. We wrote it for you, because you make such an impact on the lives of your workforce—an awesome responsibility that deserves all the help and support it can get.

Acknowledgments

Our husbands (both engineers) are great. They care about our careers, our decisions, our "un-decisions" and us. This book would not have been possible without their patience, support and ideas. Thank you, Mike and Barry.

We are both lucky to be moms. Our kids' support, excitement and cheerleading gave us a never-ending stream of encouragement. Lindsey, thanks for your patience on all those nights when I said, "Just give me ten more minutes—I'll be right there." Travis, Shelby, Matt and Kellie, thanks for bringing such joy into my life. Your successful, happy lives remind me of what matters most.

This book came alive because of the many wonderful friends, siblings (one of us has a twin who was a great and faithful reader and critic), and professional colleagues who thought with us and fought with us as we outlined the main concepts of this book.

Special thanks to Nancy Breuer, who helped give us a common voice, and to Tara Mello, who was indispensable and was the first to say, "You've got a book here." We were fortunate to have Diana Koch, who provided the critical supervisor perspective, and Marilyn Greist and Cindy Miller, who brought a never-ending stream of creativity and support. Tracy Mitchell, our illustrator, captured through art what was in our minds. Her illustrations brought our words to life. Matt Evans, our Web master, lent us his skills and know-how so we can stay in touch with all our readers.

No book comes to life without a support team. We would not be where we are without our eagle eye, Lynne Kleeger, or our artistic eye, Liliana Gallelli. Finally, we need to acknowledge the great ideas that came to us from Milo Sindell, Katherine Reynolds, Mary Ammerman, Pamela Janke and Stan Bass.

More kudos to Steve Piersanti and his talented and dedicated band of professionals at Berrett-Koehler, who told it like it was and is, who *know* their stuff and *do* their stuff terrifically well. Steve can tell you how much more work you have to do—when you thought you were finished—and actually make you excited about doing it. Truly, you have all become partners in this effort. Thanks.

A tremendous thanks in advance to those whose work just begins when the writing is finished: our crackerjack team of marketing professionals and our extended family, the talented and steadfast Career Systems International team. Grateful thanks to Kay, Nanci, Yolanda, Marilyn, Jill, Lenore, Judy, Alan, Rosalind, Janis, Tenora, Mike, Helen, Art, Ray, Bev B. and Marc.

Finally, Bev thanks Sharon for never ever leaving well enough alone (groan) and for hanging on to the "we can make this better" philosophy until . . . it really was.

Sharon thanks Bev for being ever true to her commitments and for partnering as only a genuine professional and friend can.

INTRODUCTION

―――――

A.J.'s Exit

I quit.
I'm giving you my notice.
I found another opportunity.
I've accepted another offer.
Can we talk?

If any of the above strike fear in your heart or make your stomach sink, you are not alone. Anyone managing or supervising others, whether in a skyscraper, a coffee shop, or a volunteer group, reacts with dismay to statements like these. Especially when the people saying them are critical to your team.

By "critical" we don't mean just your top performers. We mean the people who are necessary to the success of your unit and your peace of mind. They are the good, talented employees that you simply cannot afford to lose. They are your stars.

Like A.J. A critical and solid performer. Making a competitive salary. Working for an organization that has a good future. On the next page, you'll find the exit memo from A.J. to the department manager and the manager's manager.

Read it. Underline the points that resonate. Could this happen to you?

INTEROFFICE MEMO

To: Carlos and Madeleine
From: A.J.
Re: Exit Interview

Today I received the Exit Interview form from Human Resources. I put the form aside. It didn't ask the right questions for me, so I'm writing this letter instead. I still feel bad about leaving our company. I liked working with you and our team. I just couldn't stay. Maybe my letter will help you to prevent this from happening again.

Carlos, I think you are an effective manager. You complete projects, achieve goals and accomplish everything through a talented group of employees. All of these were rewarding while I was still learning our business. Unfortunately, you got too busy to pay attention to the little things. Like saying good morning. Or trying to delegate assignments so that we could learn something new. Instead, under pressure, you always took the shortcut and gave the work to people who had experience. How can anyone grow if they don't have a chance to learn? We talked a few times about the chance for me to attend training classes, or to prepare and present our plan to the executives, but those chances never materialized. A year later, I began to understand that they never would happen.

Madeleine, I have always admired you. You provide great leadership and direction to Carlos and our team and our colleagues in the division. When I first joined the company four years ago, I was so impressed by our mission statement and corporate values. I hoped to have a long and happy career here.

I have to say I became disillusioned over time. I really decided to leave in the last two months. We worked so hard on that last project. I rescheduled my vacation. The whole team put in extra hours. We produced quality work on time, achieving all objectives. Then the company decided not to implement the plan. I could even understand that decision, knowing how fast change happens around here and in any business. But no one took the time to let us know. We continued with implementation for three weeks before we heard rumors that the project was canceled. We would have understood if you'd come to our area and told us. Instead we were angry and disappointed.

It is true that my new position pays a higher salary, but I'm not leaving for money. I need to work in a place where I can make a contribution and people treat each other with respect. Sadly, my work didn't seem to make a difference here.

Thank you for all you taught me. Please remember that thoughtful planning, honest and continuous communication and basic human respect go a long way with your employees.

I wish you every success.

Have you ever had an employee like A.J.? A solid contributor, someone you really could not afford to lose, but who left anyway? How many times have you said:

"If I'd only known."

"Why didn't they tell me?"

"Why didn't I see that coming?"

"The answer was easy. I could have fixed that."

"Why didn't I ask?"

Well, don't knock your head against a wall. Scan the 26 chapters in this book. Pick out a few that capture you because you have a hunch they relate directly to you or to one of your people.

And if you have no idea what would really keep your talent, then start with the first chapter, **Ask: What Keeps You?**

And if you're not convinced that this problem is in your area of responsibility, then read Chapter Two, **Buck: It Stops Here.**

Chapter 1

 **A**SK

What Keeps You?

They never asked. —A.J.

The brainstorming continues. Human resource specialists and senior level leaders spend countless hours pondering the question. Special task forces and consultants conduct research. They benchmark other organizations in related industries, all in a quest for the answer. Eventually, they create *the* strategy, the master plan. What are they trying to do? Hold on to key talent—the employees, knowledge workers, associates, technical and/or functional specialists who do the work and keep your company successful.

All that effort, time and money may be well spent. But we have noticed that the obvious is often overlooked. Has anyone *asked* your employees what keeps them at your company? Has anyone asked what might lure key talent away? Have you? If not, why not? Why do we ask great questions in exit interviews, but neglect asking early enough to make a difference?

Ask—So You Don't Have to Guess

When we suggest asking employees why they stay or what would keep them, we hear reactions such as: "You've got to be kidding." "Isn't that illegal?" "What if they give me an answer I don't want to hear?" We dance around this core subject for fear of putting someone on the spot or putting ideas into someone's head (as if they never thought about leaving on their own).

Some managers are afraid they will be unable to do anything anyway, so why ask? They fear that the question will raise more dust than they can settle and may cause employees to expect answers and solutions that are out of the manager's hands. And there is another reason: Time. Many managers say that their time is totally consumed by the business at hand. There is an urgency to succeed, leaving little time to listen, let alone ask. If you fall into this category, you are missing a secret of how to succeed: through asking.

The Dangers of Guessing

What if you don't ask? What if you just keep trying to guess what Tara or Mike or Marilyn really want? You will guess right sometimes. The Christmas bonus might please them all. Money can inspire loyalty and commitment for the near term. But if the key to retaining Tara is to give her a chance to learn something new, whereas Mike wants to telecommute, how could you ever guess that? Ask—so you don't have to guess.

Alas

A senior manager told us of an employee who was leaving his company. On her last day, the senior manager, who was upset at the loss, expressed his disappointment that she was leaving. He wished her well but said, "I wish there were something we could have done to keep you," assuming that her direct supervisor had asked what would make her stay. But the supervisor hadn't asked, and something could have been done. The employee said she would have stayed if she could have been more involved in higher-level meetings, as she felt they were vital to her goal of growing her career. It was a request that would have been easy to fill—if only he had known!

Asking has positive side effects. The person you ask will feel cared about, valued and important. Many times that leads to stronger loyalty and commitment to you and the organization. In other words, just asking the question is a retention strategy.

How to Ask

How and when do you bring up this topic? How can you increase the odds of getting honest input from your employees? There is no single way or time to ask. It could happen during a developmental or career discussion with your employees. (You do hold those, don't you?) In that context, you could simply ask: "What would make you want to stay here? What might lure you away?" Be understanding and listen actively to the answers you receive. Does the person want a chance to grow and learn, or will a promotion and big title keep him with your company? Is it something else?

see UNDERSTAND

After you listen, you need to respond. What you say is critical. Responses like "That's unrealistic" immediately halt the dialogue and your employee will be unlikely to open up again. And he or she may go so far as to start a job search.

Another Way to Ask

Maybe you are uncomfortable with the direct question, What will keep you here? And perhaps your employees are hesitant to answer. If so, ask in a more comfortable way. Try this:

TO DO . . .

✓ Think back to a time when you stayed with one organization for a fairly long time. "Long" is a relative term and may mean twenty years or three years, depending on who you are and the type of work you do. You can think about this company or a previous employer.

What kept you there? Jot down two or three major reasons why you stayed as long as you did.

This question might be easier for some employees to answer because it describes previous times in their lives and avoids current needs and wants. What kept them before is most likely to keep them on your team today.

They Dared to Ask

The Story. A high-tech company in Silicon Valley decided to ask. It asked in a different way, for a specific group of talented people, but for the same reason. It wanted to target its retention efforts, to give people what really mattered to them and thereby hang on to these employees. Here is how it worked.

The organization recognized that a group of employees was at great risk for leaving the company. The employees, who were being trained to implement a new business integration software system, would soon become hot commodities to many other companies, due to their new training and experience. Calls from headhunters came in even during the early stages of their training. The company realized quickly that it could lose key assets if it wasn't careful; in other companies eight out of ten newly trained specialists left during or immediately following implementation. Most reportedly left because they were offered big bucks by the competition or consulting firms.

The Method. Rather than guess at retention remedies and approaches, the company began by asking employees exactly what would keep them and what would lure them away. Three external consultants conducted confidential interviews with each of the individuals in the "at-risk" group. The responses were candid and provided exactly the information the company was seeking. People knew what they wanted, and it was not always money.

The Findings. Many people said they wanted the opportunity to do "meaningful work" after the implementation project was completed, rather than return to what they had been doing before. Some wanted another team experience rather than individual work. Others wanted another challenge and opportunity to stretch and grow.

The Outcome. Once management knew what individuals wanted, it was able to partner with key employees to find those opportunities inside the company. One and a half years later only one member of this talented group of employees had left the organization, and it was because she wanted to try the consulting arena. Against all odds, the others stayed despite financially lucrative offers from other organizations.

TO DO . . .

✓ Ask each employee what keeps him or her at your company or your department. Make a card or note in your computer for every employee's answer. Every month, review the cards and ask yourself what you've done for that employee that relates to his or her needs. This will serve as a written reminder of what is important to your employees and what you need to do to make sure they remain a part of your team.

Why Most Say They Stay

Our research confirms what many others have learned about the most common reasons employees remain at a company (and what will help retain them). The items come up again and again throughout every industry and at every level. Here are the most common reasons people stay, listed in order of popularity and frequency (Note: 90 percent of respondents listed at least one of the first three items among the top three or four reasons they stayed):

1. Career growth, learning and development
2. Exciting work and challenge
3. Meaningful work, making a difference and a contribution
4. Great people
5. Being part of a team
6. Good boss
7. Recognition for work well done
8. Fun on the job
9. Autonomy, sense of control over my work
10. Flexibility—for example, in work hours and dress code
11. Fair pay and benefits
12. Inspiring leadership
13. Pride in organization, its mission and quality of product
14. Great work environment
15. Location
16. Job security
17. Family-friendly
18. Cutting-edge technology

How do your employees' answers match or differ from the list? Find out what truly matters to them by asking. Then create customized, innovative approaches to retaining your talent.

TO DO . . .

✓ Look back at the list and ask yourself which of these you can offer. Check all those that you believe are largely within your control. If our hunch is correct, you will find that many more are in your control than you thought.

Beyond "Why Did You Stay . . ."

Most of this chapter focuses on the questions "What kept you?" and "Why did you stay?" But there are many other questions you might ask to try to keep your employees. The answers to these and similar questions will help you customize your retention efforts.

Sample Questions

✓ Are you recognized for your accomplishments?
✓ Does your immediate manager support you in matching your skills and desires to your career goals?
✓ Are you challenged in your day-to-day work?
✓ Is the training you want available to you?
✓ Has your manager helped you develop a career action plan?
✓ Does your manager give you regular, candid feedback?
✓ What are you struggling with all the time?
✓ What would make your life easier?

Consider selecting three or four of these and asking the same ones every quarter. It's a great way to keep your own retention check in operation.

At Bain & Co. if someone is unhappy, managers push the pause button and stop the action. They ask: Would this person prefer to work on different projects? Is the work-family balance out of whack? Is compensation fair? If the employee is running to an opportunity, rather than away from Bain, the company gives the employee their full support.[1]

BOTTOM LINE

Stop guessing what will keep your stars home and happy. If you need to, have someone else do the asking for you. It might be a human resources professional, an outside consultant or a manager from another unit in your organization. Or you might ask orally or in written form, as in a quick survey, where answers can be written or e-mailed. Perhaps you could ask in an anonymous way by having a third party collect the answers, group them and give them to you. Or take our favorite approach—ask the questions yourself, one-on-one, with your employees. This may be all you need to do.

It doesn't matter so much where, when or how you ask—just ASK!

_____

Chapter 2

BUCK

It Stops Here

I think my manager actually could have kept me. But I don't think he ever saw it as his job.

—A.J.

When we ask supervisors and managers how they keep good people, many immediately respond, "With money." Research suggests that 89 percent of managers truly believe it's largely about the money.[1] These managers put the responsibility for keeping key people squarely in the hands of senior management. They blame organizational policies or pay scales for the loss of talent.

Well, the truth is, *you matter most.* If you are a manager at any level, a front-line supervisor or a project leader, you actually have more power than anyone else to keep your best employees. Why? Because the factors that drive employee satisfaction and commitment are largely within your control. And the factors that satisfy employees are the ones that keep them on your team. Those factors haven't changed much over the past 25 years. Many researchers[2] who have studied retention agree on what satisfies people and therefore influences them to stay: meaningful, challenging work, a chance to learn and grow, fair compensation, a good work environment, recognition and respect. Don't you want those things?

It's Up to You

A good boss who cares about employees will help talented people find those things in their work. We're not saying you travel this road alone. Senior management and your organization's policies, systems and culture have an impact on your ability to keep talented people. You may have human resources professionals who can help support your efforts. And yet, because of what research tells us about *why* people leave their jobs and organizations, *you* still have the greatest power (and responsibility) for keeping your talented employees.

Alas

There's nothing I can do about our brain drain. The competition is offering more money and better perks. We don't stand a chance.

—Manager, retail pharmacy

You do stand a chance. Your relationship with employees is key to their satisfaction and decisions to stay or leave. One study found that 50 percent of work life satisfaction is determined by the relationship a worker has with his or her immediate boss.[3] In other words, *you matter.*

> *Insofar as employee commitment exists, it is to the boss, to the team, and to the project. That's different from loyalty, which previously was to the name on the building or to the brand. Therefore, any retention strategy must be driven by individual managers and supervisors, not just the folks in human resources.*
>
> —President, Aon Consulting Institute

On the Line

Most of you are in charge of certain assets. You are held accountable for protecting those assets and for growing them. Today, your most critical assets are *people*, not *property*. Outstanding people give you and your organization a competitive advantage. Regardless of the job market, you no doubt want to hold on to your best. How are you doing that?

Are you responsible for selecting and keeping talented people? We heard of a CEO who charged $30,000 to a manager's operating budget because he needlessly lost a talented person. The buck really did stop there! We're not suggesting that managers be punished when their people are promoted or move on to learn something new. You will inevitably lose some talented employees occasionally, especially as they pursue their career dreams. But we do recommend that managers be held accountable for being good managers and for creating a retention culture where people feel motivated, cared about and rewarded.

Calling All Managers of Managers

If managers report to you, do you hold them accountable for the team they manage? How? You've probably heard the maxim that busy people do what is *inspected*, not necessarily what is *expected*. Honest efforts to keep good people should be expected because those people build your business. If you do manage others, you may need to invent some inspection or accountability mechanisms. Here are some options.

TO DO . . .

Devise a Retention Commitment Process

✓ List all 26 strategies in this book (use Table of Contents for summary) on a paper or electronic form. Or have your team narrow the 26 down to 10 or so that they think are the most appropriate for your culture.

✓ Ask each of your managers or supervisors to commit to two that they are willing to implement within the next six months. Have them circle and initial those two and return a copy of the form to you.

✓ Six months later, ask them to return their retention commitment forms to you with a description of what they did for each of the strategies they committed to.

or

Create a Retention Appraisal

✓ List all chapter headings from this book on a form. (Or limit it to the ones you select, as above.)
✓ Ask each of your managers to rate themselves on each strategy, using a one-to-five scale.
✓ Then (if you dare . . . and if they dare) ask them to distribute blank forms to their direct reports. Let their direct reports tell it like it is by rating them on a one-to-five scale.
✓ Reward those who get serious, and have a chat with those who don't.

Want one more?

TO DO . . .

✓ Send the following memo (edit it to your liking) to your direct reports. Tape it to the front of this book. Hold a meeting in two weeks, and talk about their reactions.

To: Team
From: Your Manager
RE: Retaining the Talented People on Our Team

This memo is written to everyone who manages people. *I need your help.* I am concerned about the war for talent that I have been reading about and how it affects our work group. We want to be the best at what we do. We want not only to survive but to thrive in the coming years. Our success depends on our ability to recruit and retain the very finest people. Our talent *is* our competitive edge.

I think your role is critical. While pay, perks, and benefits do matter, people stay or leave based on other factors, many of which are actually in *your* hands.

So here is my request. Read this book. As you read it, think about what you are currently doing to retain the talent on your team. Pick just one retention strategy from the A–Z list provided in this book. Give it a try. See what happens. I want to know about it.

I'm calling a series of monthly meetings. We'll all talk about the strategies that work and those that don't. Read the "ALAS" stories too. I think we'll have some of our own to add to the list. Let's talk about why they happened—and how to prevent more of them.

First meeting: Conference Room A at 8:30.

If you're not a manager of managers, hold yourself accountable. Look at the talented people you are responsible for leading and for keeping in the organization. Decide which strategies in this book you could use right away to increase the odds that they will stay.

So They Go

So what? Can't you just replace them? You might be able to replace your key people, but at what cost? Multiple research studies suggest that the cost of replacing key people runs between 70 and 200 percent of the person's annual salary. One study found that the top three reasons for implementing retention programs in organizations are:[4]

see NUMBERS

1. Losing an employee costs between 6 and 18 months' pay.
2. Hi-tech workers, professionals and managers cost twice as much as other employees to replace.
3. Many hidden costs are incurred through lost sales and lost customers.

Even if you can afford to replace them, will you be able to find talented replacements? The U.S. Bureau of Labor Statistics projects that there will be 151 million jobs by the year 2006 and 141 million people employed. Many of those workers will be working two jobs.[5] Alan Greenspan declared in February 1999 that the limiting factor to the U.S. continued economic growth is *people*. He said that there are simply not enough people to feed the economic machine.

Meanwhile we read about Amazon.com and other organizations being sued for talent theft. The message is clear. Talented people are scarce and will continue to be scarce. If you have them working on your team, you had better try your best to keep them.

TO DO . . .

✓ Pay attention to the research about what keeps people. Note that most of the proven strategies are within your control.

✓ If you manage managers, hold them accountable for hiring and keeping good people in the organization. Establish clear expectations and measure results. People will do what is *inspected* more than what is *expected*.

✓ Do just one thing. Choose a chapter in this book and try a strategy. See how it works. Modify and adapt it to fit your needs. Then try another.

BOTTOM LINE

The buck really does stop here. You have the power to greatly influence your talented employees' decisions about staying on your team. Show that you care about them and their needs. Remember them. Notice them. Listen to them. Thank them. Love them or lose them.

Chapter 3

CAREERS

Support Growth

I guess I just never saw a future for myself here. I don't mean I ever expected a path all laid out, but I did expect that somewhere, someone would talk to me about my future.

—A.J.

A.J. probably had a future with this employer, but if that future was a secret in senior managers' minds only, it had no power to influence A.J.'s decisions. If there has never been a discussion about an employee's career, your chances of keeping that person are greatly diminished.

Alas

A young graphic designer complained that he had given 110 percent to his job in a small advertising company and now was disappointed that graphic designers with less tenure were being given better assignments. He felt taken for granted! He considered going to his boss to talk about the situation, but he simply resigned without saying a word.

If that manager had asked some good questions, he may have discovered career-related currencies other than money that he could offer. Perhaps all the manager needed to do was show interest in his employee's career.

So What's a Manager To Do?

Far too many managers steer clear of career conversations. Which of the following barriers keep you from opening up this topic?

✓ No one, let alone me, knows what the future holds.
✓ It is just not the right time.
✓ I'm not prepared.
✓ I wouldn't know what to say.
✓ We've just reorganized. It will be a while before anyone knows anything about career possibilities.
✓ I would never open something I couldn't close.
✓ I don't know enough about what's outside my department to offer advice.
✓ I don't want anyone blaming me if they don't get what they want.
✓ Why should I help? Nobody ever helped me.

What your employees really want is two-way conversations with you to talk about their abilities, choices and ideas. They want you to listen. They may not expect you to have the answers, but they expect and really want to have the dialogue.

You construct the pipeline for the flow of talent in your organization. When your people feel that you care about developing them, they believe the organization cares. This chapter provides the basics on building your talent pipeline. Several steps need to be taken continually to support your employees' search for a good career fit.

Depth Over Breadth

The primary objective of career conversations is that you listen for information that will tell you more about your employees. It is frequently difficult for employees to talk about their skills, values and interests. Open up a dialogue that gives you and your employees an opportunity to become more aware of who they are both professionally and personally.

To get them talking, ask questions that help them to think more deeply about their unique skills, interests and values. The toughest part is to listen while they answer, as a diligent researcher would. Probe, inquire and discover more.

see UNDERSTAND

TO DO . . .

Try asking these and then probe each answer more deeply:

✓ What makes you unique in this organization?
✓ Tell me about an accomplishment of which you are particularly proud.
✓ What are your most important values? Which values are met and not met at work?
✓ If you had to choose among working with people, data, things, or ideas, which mixture would make you the happiest? Why?

Feedback Is Vital

Helping your employees to reflect on their own reputations, on the feedback they've gotten from others, and on the areas they need to develop is essential. Your frequent feedback is critical.

Alas (almost)

Recently, a senior HR person stopped to say hi to someone who started on the same day she did . . . about six months ago. He was considered a fast-track high-potential and was getting excellent press from very high up in the organization. She said, "Hi, how's it going?" He shrugged his shoulders and said it was going okay, he guessed, but he wasn't really happy and didn't feel he was making any progress. She was shocked to find that no one had ever told this guy what a great job he was doing. When she told him WHO was impressed by him, his face lit up. He had no idea he was valued.

see TRUTH

Think back to that last performance review you gave. It probably was based on past performance and connected to that employee's raise. Development feedback is different. It is future-oriented and focused on areas where the employee can improve.

Employees want specific feedback with examples of their performance and the effect on their future goals. Have them seek out people in their career audience at all levels who will give them a more realistic self-portrait that will help them develop faster and smarter.

TO DO . . .

Try preparing for this conversation by asking yourself:

✓ Which tasks does he/she most need to focus on to maximize his/her contribution?
✓ How do you really see his/her potential to grow based on what you identified on his/her most recent performance appraisal?
✓ What is his/her reputation among coworkers?
✓ How will you begin this conversation?

Think about all the awkward conversations you've had with employees whose career goals are simply out of sync with reality given their strengths and weaknesses. Remember, *the absence of honest feedback kept them out of sync!* Employees continually tell us that they want straight talk. Want to keep them? Level with them.

Data, Data Everywhere

Helping your people consider their options means helping them look beyond your department to detect shifts and changes that might impact their careers. You will need to sniff out your company's growth areas and limitations as well as changes in the skills the industry will require.

Alas

Lenore was exactly what our organization needed. She was young and wanted to use her technical as well as managerial skills, wanted to develop business, and in fact had already brought some in. She decided to look for a new job when she heard that there were some changes coming in our organization and she realized she didn't know what would happen to her. She said that her first manager was great at coaching and keeping her in the loop, but that she had recently been moved to work for another manager who had shown no interest in her career. So with the threat of impending change, and a manager who didn't seem to care, she took an offer at a small start-up company. She was clear that it was not the salary and benefits that drew her. It was the hope of a better manager, one who would keep her 'in the loop' and care about her career. The exit interview lasted 90 minutes. I asked her if she would reconsider. She declined.

—Human resources manager

Clearly, a good career conversation with her new manager could have influenced Lenore's decision to look around.

TO DO . . .

Ask yourself if your employees know:

✓ The major economic, political and social changes taking place that will have the greatest effect on your organization?
✓ The opportunities and problems ahead?
✓ What areas are changing the most within your industry?
✓ How their profession will be different in the next two years? Five years?
✓ What really counts for success in your organization?
✓ Which trade publications, journals and organization newsletters provide information on industry and business trends?

You don't have to take this all on your own shoulders. But you do have to ensure that they know what's going on in your organization. By suggesting others who can provide additional perspectives on these and other issues, you open channels for your employees and pull them closer to the key business needs of the organization. Have you done this lately?

More Choices = More Choices!

see GOALS

Helping your employees consider multiple career goals *while* they grow within their current position is a key element in development. When employees analyze their potential development goals in terms of business needs and the strategic intent of the organization, everyone wins.

Caution! The employee is still primarily responsible for his or her career. Our suggestions do not mean *telling* the person what to do. Instead, offer choices for employees to analyze and consider. This is important (but sometimes difficult); for generations, the only acceptable career direction has been up. But there are at least six ways employees can move their careers along. Discuss with your employees what success means to them; it's a conversation they may never have had. Ask, for example, "In your career, has anyone ever explored these job options with you?"

✓ **Lateral** (moving across) involves a change in job, but not necessarily a change in the level of responsibility.
✓ **Exploratory** (investigating possibilities) requires answering questions like "What else can I do?"
✓ **Enrichment** (growing in place) recommends that the current job can be fertile ground for growth and learning.
✓ **Realignment** (moving down) reconciles the demands of work with other priorities. Realignment also can imply getting back to the line job you loved before you got into management.
✓ **Relocation** (moving out) means leaving the organization when the work simply cannot match a person's skills, interests or values.
✓ **Vertical** (moving up) describes the traditional way to move—up. However, "up" is in short supply in most organizations.

You can give your employees permission to discover the possibilities based on what turns them on, what they value and what they can contribute to the organization.

The more career goals your employee identifies, the better. *The biggest career frustrations (and the most exits) occur when an employee's only goal is thwarted.*

TO DO . . .

Ask your employees these questions. All are critical to goal setting.

✓ Do you have enough information about the organization's current activities and plans to select several career goals?
✓ How can you get the information you need?
✓ Have you considered all available directions in selecting your career options?

✓ Do your options adequately cover a variety of scenarios?
✓ Should you select more career options?
✓ Are your goals compatible with organizational goals and plans?

Once you have helped your employees look at options so that all their plans are not caught up in the vertical mindset, you can encourage them to identify the skills, development opportunities and knowledge areas required for each alternative.

BOTTOM LINE

Keeping your employees on a continual path of growing, developing and adding new skills will help you keep your competitive edge. You must help them discover the inevitable barriers that will get in their way. But they must overcome them and do the work. Help them build alliances and relationships to meet their goals.

Any organization that ignores the ambitions of good people can't expect to keep them.

 **IGNITY**

Show Respect

I generally felt respected in this organization, but that was not the case for everyone. I remember feeling embarrassed when a manager humiliated his secretary in front of several of her colleagues. It was so disrespectful and no one said or did anything about it.

—A.J.

If we interviewed your employees and asked them what kind of boss you are, what would they say? Would they say that you are smart, dedicated, motivating, hard charging? How about results-oriented, demanding or fun to work with? Just as you tolerate a range of behaviors from your employees, so too your employees will accept *you* as you are, no doubt less than perfect but doing your best. The one behavior that talented people seldom tolerate for long is disrespect. If you wish to keep them, it is absolutely critical that you respect them, recognize each of their unique qualities and then demonstrate your respect in consistent, undeniable ways. Remember to treat them as you would like to be treated.

Alas

We lost one of our most important paralegal assistants. Every attorney in our office counted on her and we were shocked to see her go. In her exit interview she said it was not the pay or perks that caused her to seek a new job. It was the daily, weekly indignities that she suffered while trying to do her best in this job. Her performance review (and possible raise) had been overlooked for the past six months; her request to join an association of paralegals still lay on her boss's desk after six weeks; she was denied attendance at a free seminar that would have benefited the firm, because they couldn't free her up; she had not been thanked for her hard work and excellent results; her boss grunted and vented and took out his frustrations on her without giving it a second thought. She finally left the firm because she did not feel respected or valued, but did feel used and demeaned. And everyone noticed."

—Attorney, major law firm

Could that happen at your workplace? Have you, or has someone you know, ever left for reasons like that?

Different Strokes

You cannot respect and honor others unless you respect (even celebrate) the differences between people. Can you imagine how ineffective (and boring) your team would be if everyone thought the same, looked the same, believed the same, had the same talents? Most of us readily accept the notion that diversity of talent and perspective strengthens a work group and contributes to excellent results. Yet if we are honest, we admit that differences also get in the way. The hard truth is that many of us more often *tolerate* than *celebrate* differences.

The Museum of Tolerance in Los Angeles welcomes its visitors in a unique way. As a tour group forms in the lobby, they are invited into a waiting room that admits them into the museum. Our tour guide said to us, "Notice that there are two doors through which you may enter this museum. One is marked prejudiced *and the other is marked* unprejudiced. *You may enter through whichever door represents you." There was a long pause as people pondered what they should do, which door to choose. Finally a man bravely stepped forward and turned the knob on the door marked* unprejudiced. *A few stepped forward to follow him, while the rest of us watched. He turned the knob, looked a little confused and then turned red with embarrassment as he realized the door was locked. We could only enter the museum through the door marked* prejudiced.

—Sharon Jordan-Evans

What is your reaction to that story? Which door would you have chosen? What would your reaction be to the locked door? It is important for most of us to take a good look at our preferences and prejudices; we all have them. They pop up in front of us when we mentor and coach, promote, reward, punish and hire (research shows we are most apt to hire someone like ourselves). Once you take note of your prejudices, you can begin to see the impact they might have on your employees.

He is young and I am older. He is a man and I am a woman. He is west coast and I am east coast. He is a runner and I am overweight. Where is our common ground and how will we work together?

—Marketing manager, confiding in a coworker

The first step in leveraging differences is to take a good look at your own beliefs. How much do you respect people very different from yourself? Do you value what they bring to your team? How badly do you want them to stay?

TO DO . . .

✓ Analyze your attitudes and prejudices. Admit to your leanings toward or away from those with different:

- Skin color
- Status
- Education
- Height or weight
- Title
- Accent
- Geographic origin
- Talent
- _____ (add one)

- Personality
- Age
- Job function
- Gender
- Lifestyle
- Sexual orientation

✓ Notice how your prejudices play out at work. Whom did you last promote? Whom do you tend to ignore, praise less often, be friendly with or not?

✓ *Decide* to change. Practice fairness and consciously avoid discriminating in the old familiar ways. Your employees will notice.

✓ Leverage the differences among your employees. Roosevelt Thomas, diversity consultant and author, defines diversity as the maximum utilization of talent in the workforce. Appreciate and utilize individual strengths, styles and talents.

I do not like this person. I must get to know him better.

—Abraham Lincoln

When people get their backs up about diversity, often they're resisting what they see as an effort to change how they feel. Valuing differences does not force you to change how you feel. It's about how you act at work to keep good employees.

In the Mood?

Honoring others and treating them with dignity and respect may mean managing your moods. Have you ever worked for someone with roller-coaster moods? You know, one day he's up, the next he's *way* down. While it is human to have ups and downs, it is grown up to manage those moods so that they do not hurt others. Some call moods that have run amok *sloppy moods*. They are simply uncontrolled. Whatever is felt comes spilling out and slops all over employees (or family). The results can be embarrassment, hurt, anger, humiliation and loss of dignity.

see JERK

TO DO . . .

✓ If you are guilty of sloppy moods, take notice and take control. Get away from others while you work through your difficulties. Go to your room; take a *time out*.

✓ If you happen to slop on someone, apologize. To err is human and most people appreciate an apology; it is a sign of respect.

✓ If you have a serious emotional problem, consider seeking help from a professional or your organization's Employee Assistance Program (EAP).

Are They Invisible?

My previous boss never said hello to me. He would walk right past me in the hall as if I did not exist, or was invisible. He did say hello to every vice president. My new boss treats me with respect. I feel like she values me as a person, even though her job level is above mine. I love working here.

—Bank teller

When employees talk about the disrespect that drove them out the door to a new job, they sometimes refer to this feeling of invisibility. It's as if they felt so insignificant that they were invisible. You might be simply lost in thought when you pass your employees in the hall and fail to acknowledge them. But they will notice and may feel less than honored or respected.

TO DO . . .

✓ Notice your employees. Pay attention as you walk down the halls and say hello to them by name.

✓ Smile, shake hands, greet your employees and introduce them to others, even those of higher rank. They will feel honored and definitely not invisible.

Trust Me

Some say that trust is a gift. Others say it must be earned. Still others refuse to trust anyone at all. Andy Grove, chairman of Intel, even wrote a book called *Only the Paranoid Survive.* Great title, but in practice it is a tough way to live!

What we know is that when you trust your employees, most will be trustworthy. They will feel honored and respected when you trust them with important tasks and heavy responsibilities and when you let them do things their way. The opposite, of course, is true as well. When you fail to trust them, they will often feel dishonored, disrespected and undervalued. And you can bet they will leave when a better opportunity presents itself.

If you doubt this, think about a time in your career when you had a boss who trusted you implicitly. Trusted you to excel. Trusted you with information or assets. How did you feel? What was your level of commitment to the boss or the organization as a result?

Alas

He simply could not learn to trust us. It was as if he thought that we were all out to get him and in the end it was almost a self-fulfilling prophecy. We knew we were worthy of his trust and yet we almost began to feel guilty as he micro-managed us and constantly looked over our shoulders. We had to account for every minute of our time and every nickel we spent. Finally it was just too demeaning. The entire team decided to find other employment and a boss who trusted us.

—Director, engineering firm

If only the boss had realized whom he had on his team. They were truly not out to get him—they were just trying to do their jobs. To trust someone implicitly shows tremendous respect for that person.

TO DO . . .

✓ Check out your own ability to trust others. Do you tend to see trust as a gift or demand evidence of trustworthiness before you give it?

✓ Try trusting your employees. Say you trust them, act like you trust them and *really* trust them. Give them responsibility and then let them carry it out!

What's Fair is Fair

Talented workers will leave a boss who is perceived to be unfair. Unfair treatment translates to disrespect in many employees' minds. Check out your communication approach and your actions with your employees. How do they view the decisions and changes that you make? What seems fair or unfair to them? Do you honor their ideas and do you care about their reactions? If you don't, you will lose them.

Anybody Home?

Sometimes busy bosses seem almost unreachable. Unless the sky is falling (by their definition), it is virtually impossible to get their attention. An employee wants to leave early on Friday for his son's baseball game and asks you on the Monday before. Another employee needs your okay to attend a conference in two months. A third employee's wife has been hospitalized with a life-threatening illness. What do you do? Ideally you respond quickly in all three cases.

Unfortunately, too many busy bosses tell the first and second employees that they will get back to them but never do. The employees feel unimportant and disrespected and have to either nag for an answer or forget the whole thing (but they never really do). And what about the third employee? What does the busy boss do about that situation? Too often nothing. Treating an employee with dignity means acknowledging how difficult and unique this life situation is.

My mother was dying of cancer and lived 1,000 miles away. I was a wreck at work, unable to concentrate and feeling so guilty about not being with her. My boss took me into his office and told me to take as much time as I needed to go and be with my mother in her final days. I will never forget that act. I felt so valued and respected by him and my commitment to that organization soared.

—Secretary, consulting firm

TO DO . . .

- ✓ Listen to your employees' wants and needs. Even if they seem small or insignificant, they are clearly important to them.
- ✓ Respond to their requests in a timely manner. Don't wait for them to nag you.
- ✓ Be aware and take steps to help employees in times of need. They will pay you back a thousandfold.

BOTTOM LINE

Respecting others may seem easy enough. After all, it's really just an attitude, isn't it? It is true that attitudes and beliefs are at the core of showing respect and honoring others. But behaviors and actions are involved too. Check out your beliefs about differences and audit your actions. Listen to your employees, respond to them and—bottom line—treat them as you would like to be treated: with respect and dignity.

Chapter 5

ENRICH

Energize the Job

The job just became ho-hum. I mean, I was good at it, my customers loved my work, my appraisals were great, but after a while none of that mattered. I was just plain bored and I saw no way out.

—A.J.

Something is missing. Where did the joy go? What happened to the sense of personal change and growth? When did the feeling of new challenges change to a feeling of routine activities? When did the stimulation of opportunity become the predictability of sameness?

It Can Happen to Anyone

Unfortunately, your most valued employees are the most likely to suffer this sense of job discontent. By definition, they are savvy, creative, self-propelled and energetic. They need stimulating work, opportunities for personal challenge and growth, and a contributing stake in the organizational action. If good workers find the job with your company no longer provides these necessities, they will decide they have outgrown the place and they will leave for a job that can stretch them with new challenges.

Some employees, perhaps not the obvious stars but people with solid potential, suffer discontent yet stay on the job. Instead of leaving for the next challenge, they find ways to disengage. Their departure is psychological rather than physical. It shows up in counterproductive activities that range from absenteeism to mediocre performance. These individuals simply withhold their energy and effort, figuring, "What's the point anyway?"

Thus there are two kinds of employee response to job discontentment: departure and disengagement. Either way, you lose human capital vital to the success of your unit and your company—a preventable loss. Employees who depart or disengage because they are not content in their current jobs are telling you that *something is lacking in the work itself.* The job may provide good pay, enjoyable and respected coworkers, adequate security, appropriate benefits and other important aspects. It may be with an excellent company doing important work. However, the day-to-day elements of getting the work done may not provide the stimulation, growth, future possibilities or current sense of achievement that make an employee want to stay and to contribute wholeheartedly.

Alas

I had been doing the same work for seven years when my organization decided to diversify and expand the business in a new direction. I met with my boss to tell him that I would love to learn about the new side of the business and maybe expand my job to include at least some work in the new arena. I wasn't sure how it could all fit, but I knew I wanted something new and exciting in my day-to-day work life. When I raised the topic, he responded curtly, "The team has already been chosen to do this new work. We need you to keep doing what you're doing." That was the end of our discussion. I left the organization six months later.

—Claims adjuster, insurance company

The Enriched Get Richer

One of the most effective ways to develop improvements in the job itself is *job enrichment*. That means structuring ways in which employees can get the growth, challenge and renewal they seek without leaving their current job or organization. Change is the key, and it may occur in what is done (content) or how it is done (process). Job enrichment allows employees to take on different tasks and responsibilities or to accomplish them in ways that promote personal autonomy and creativity.

An enriched job:

✓ Requires and values quality work
✓ Gives an employee room to initiate, create and implement new ideas
✓ Promotes setting and achieving personal and group goals
✓ Allows employees to see their contribution to an end product or goal
✓ Challenges employees to expand their knowledge and capabilities and to grow in new directions
✓ Has a future beyond itself

Harley-Davidson's Kansas City plant managed to increase employee input and establish new experiences for workers at the same time when it asked line workers to take an active part in building a better motorcycle. Worker-designed items now in use at the plant include:

✓ *Carts that swivel 360 degrees and rise to various heights to suit each worker carrying parts to and from stations*
✓ *Special wheels for mounting motorcycle frames so that welders can easily reach every corner*
✓ *A power paint striping device that achieves more consistency than the previous hand painting of Harley's famous stripes*

Also, incentive bonuses are now linked to performance and production, and employees are taking key roles in planning, budgeting and purchasing.[1]

A job can be as neatly tailored to a worker's peculiar goals and requirements as a pair of Levis to an on-line customer's imperfect physique.

—David Ulrich and David Sturm

How to Get Enriched Quick

If enrichment is so beneficial, why isn't it a standard part of every job? One good reason is that every job and every employee is different. What enriches one employee is different from what enriches the next. Courtney finds the predictability of her job devastating. Marco is tired of being told how to do his audit reports. Lindsey sees that her computer programs meet the needs of her superiors but has no idea how they are used by the company. How do you tailor job enrichment to individuals and their needs? Ask them.

see ASK

TO DO . . .

Try the following questions to help people probe their work lives for possibilities of enrichment:

- ✓ Do you know how your job is important to the company?
- ✓ What skills do you use on the job? What talents do you have that you don't use?
- ✓ What about your job do you find challenging? Rewarding?
- ✓ In what areas would you like increased responsibility for your current tasks?
- ✓ What would you like to be doing in the next three to five years?
- ✓ In what ways would you like your job changed?

The idea is to bring people through a thought process that allows them to think about their jobs and discover ideas for enrichment. These ideas will, and should, vary greatly from one employee to the next. Be prepared for answers about:

- ✓ Greater autonomy
- ✓ Increased feedback
- ✓ Participation in decisions about work processes
- ✓ Opportunities for teamwork
- ✓ Greater variety in tasks performed
- ✓ New challenges and learning

When an employee gets stuck for an answer, collaborate to develop ideas. Always lay out the truth about what can and cannot happen. If an employee wants to work toward a promotion that just isn't possible in the foreseeable future, be candid and move on to other ideas for more meaningful work.

It's In Control

By now you might be shaking your head and saying, "Oh great, they all want fascinating work and more money." Slow down. Plenty of actions short of miracles are in your control. Some of the very best possibilities for job enrichment are very much in the control of managers working in concert with employees who open up to them. Here are concepts that have worked for various corporate managers:

A Checklist of Enrichment Possibilities

see OPPORTUNITIES

- ✓ **Combine tasks.** The auto industry discovered long ago that an employee doing a single, small repetitive task will not be as challenged and motivated as an employee involved in a related set of tasks, such as painting and striping an entire car rather than only the trim around the wheel wells.
- ✓ **Form teams.** Self-directed work groups can make a lot of their own decisions. They can redistribute work in ways that increase variety and learning and that enhance the possibility of seeing tasks to completion.

✓ *Put employees in touch with clients.* For example, a computer systems troubleshooter might be more effective knowing the needs of real people and units rather than responding only to problems as they occur. Assign one troubleshooter to one department and make her accountable for the computer system. Give her a client. Clients can be inside or outside the organization. It's amazing how many employees never see them.

✓ *Rotate assignments.* A formal change to new responsibilities can help an employee feel challenged and valued. It also allows for acquiring important new skills that can add depth to the workforce. Do rotational assignments sound like chaos? Suggest the idea and let your employees propose the "who" and "how" part; you'll be surprised at their expertise in making it happen smoothly.

✓ *Build in feedback.* Do more than annual reviews. Find ways to develop peer review and client review opportunities. Employees want to know about their performance, and continual feedback allows them to be their own quality-control agents.

✓ *Establish widespread participation.* Employees are empowered and motivated when they take part in decisions that have an impact on their work, such as budget and hiring decisions as well as ways to organize work and schedules. Involvement is critical to allowing employees to see the big picture and to enabling them to make a contribution they find meaningful.

✓ *Nurture creativity.* Creativity seems to dwindle when unused. If employees are rarely asked to think for themselves, they lose the ability to contribute their best ideas. They simply go through the paces, undermotivated and disengaged. Managers and supervisors can help by asking for and rewarding creative ideas, by giving employees the freedom and resources to create, and by challenging employees with new assignments, tasks and learning.

✓ *Set goals.* Ideally, each employee should set enrichment goals that will increase opportunities for challenge and growth on the job. Managers can help by asking for enrichment goals each year, discussing them with groups and individuals, and setting aside time for teams and groups to hold goal-setting sessions. Such goals may include tackling new projects, developing new processes for getting work done, teaming up with others on various tasks, achieving greater autonomy in making decisions about the work, or learning new skills.

Striking Oil with Goal Setting: A large oil company used enrichment goal setting as part of its career development program by requiring each participant to set at least two enrichment goals. Those goals were presented to a planning committee where employees were helped in refining goals and establishing implementation plans. Most goals were eventually doable and acted upon![2]

Any of these ideas can work to change the nature of the job. And none means that the individual has to move away from your department or unit. They all require just three things from you: time to listen, an open mind and a willingness to give it a try.

BOTTOM LINE

Enrichment is not tricky or difficult. But it does require that you stay alert to opportunities for all employees, encourage their own thoughts and ideas and develop enrichment projects where possible. Most of all, it requires that you adopt a mindset that helps you understand that when you help a talented employee enrich his or her job, you may feel like you are losing control. In the long run, however, letting go may be the best way to encourage a valued employee to stay on board.

Chapter 6

 **F**AMILY

Get Friendly

Now this wasn't a big thing, but it certainly added to everything else. There was one time that I remember distinctly, when my child was in a soccer game and I wanted to attend. My manager made it clear that he did not approve of my leaving work early to see her game.

—A.J.

How are things at home? How are your folks? When was the last time you had a special lunch with a family member who needs more time with you? Is anyone at home complaining about not seeing enough of you?

People quit when rigid workplace rules cause unbearable family stress. Would they leave your organization over work/family conflicts? Yes. Business magazines have spent plenty of ink in recent years on the importance of developing a "family-friendly culture." But what does it really mean?

Employees are asking for a workplace that helps them balance the demands of their work and family lives, rather than forcing them to choose one over the other. Today and from now on, organizations that are not family-friendly will definitely have a harder time getting their good people to stay.

Talented employees do not have to look far to find employers that offer child care facilities or subsidies, flexible work schedules, job sharing, telecommuting, eldercare assistance (such as referral programs) and extended and creative maternity (even paternity) leave programs. Organizations with family-friendly programs give employees flexibility in how they work, when they work, and often where they work. They allow employees to meet personal responsibilities while still being productive at work.

If your organization does have these policies and perks in place, that's great. But if not, you have two options. One is to benchmark, get smart about what other organizations are offering and then go to your manager (and/or the human resources department) with information and suggestions. See if you can run these ideas up the flagpole and get some of them adopted in your organization. Whether or not you take the first option, you can take the more urgent one: become a more family-friendly manager. There are things that *you* can do to support your employees' lives outside of work (they do have them), and the result will be more dedicated workers who are less likely to stray. We recommend that you pursue both options.

What Does Family Mean and What Do They Want?

What do we mean by the word "family"? Some of you might immediately picture small children and a mom and dad. Others picture a single male caring for his aging father, a young newlywed couple or a Gen-Xer and his dog. One family-friendly strategy won't meet all of these employees' individual needs. It's critical that you take into account the different types of families in your group and then think about (and talk about) the approaches that will work best for each of them. Remember, the most accurate way to get this information quickly is simply to ask your employees.

see ASK

TO DO...

✓ Ask your employees, "What would make your life easier?" In their answers, look for small things that you, their manager, might be able to do to help. Brainstorm with your employees to create some innovative solutions to the work/family challenges.

Get Friendly

You may feel restricted by your organization's lack of family-friendly programs or policies. Yet we know that what you do (and fail to do) as a manager can mean so much to your employees as they juggle work and family. You may have tremendous opportunities to *get family-friendly* within your own work group. And much of what you can do as a manager costs you and your organization little or nothing.

Alas

Ernie was frustrated and exhausted trying to manage his work and family life. His wife worked also and they had a six-month-old baby. Ernie was one of those dads who wanted to partner with his wife in the raising of their child, so he began to flex his hours a bit to pick up the baby at childcare or take her to the doctor. His productivity and work quality remained high but his hours had dropped (from 55 to 45 a week) and looked somewhat erratic. The boss told Ernie that he simply had to return to his previous schedule, end of discussion. Even though Ernie tried to explain his needs, the boss had no time and no tolerance. Within two months Ernie had found a new job, one with a family-friendly culture and a boss who allowed him flexibility in his schedule.

Get Flexible

Ernie's boss lost a valuable employee, one who may be very costly to replace, all because he did not take the time to listen and to work with his employee toward a win-win solution. His rigidity cost him dearly. Think flexibly the next time an employee asks you for different work hours or time off to help a spouse, parent or friend. Think about the real costs of saying yes. Will productivity suffer? Will a dangerous precedent be set? Will that employee begin to take advantage of you? It is more likely that your employees will applaud (maybe silently) your open-mindedness and willingness to help a valued employee in a time of need. Remember to set clear expectations for your employees' results and hold them to those results. Then you will have room to flex when it matters.

> *Deloitte & Touche's CEO was alarmed at the high rate of turnover among its female accountants. Interviews with employees led to a flexible workplace program with an immediate return on investment: reduced attrition.[1]*

> *****

> *DuPont Corporation has created flexible work schedules to reduce its turnover rate. Employees are never questioned about why they need the flexibility. They can use it for childcare or golf—either is fine.[2]*

Even though these are corporate examples, as a manager you can no doubt implement some degree of flexibility for your team.

Get Supportive

Some managers mistakenly think that they should clearly separate themselves from their employees' personal lives. You have much more to gain by being interested in and supportive of their lives outside of work.

> *I was so excited about my daughter's singing debut at her high school. She had been taking vocal lessons, had developed a strong, beautiful voice and now was her chance to show it off. She would sing the Star Spangled Banner (without accompaniment) during the*

all-school pep rally at 1 P.M. My boss was excited for me and said, "No problem," when I asked him if I could go watch her. But here's the best part. Upon my return, with videotape in hand, he asked me how it went and asked if I would show him the tape. It was such a small thing, but meant so much to me. I proudly showed him the video and beamed as he praised my daughter. He showed support in so many ways that day.

—Receptionist, manufacturing firm

There are many ways to show support. We have heard about managers who became involved in numerous ways. As you read these approaches, think about which ones might work for you and your employees. Maybe an idea here will serve as a catalyst for another creative thought. Some managers have shown support in these ways:

✓ Allowing employees' children to come to work with them occasionally, usually to celebrate a special occasion or because of a special need

✓ Driving to an employee's house to be with her and her family following a death in the family

✓ Accompanying employees to their children's ball games and recitals

✓ Inviting an employee and his or her parents, relatives or children to lunch

✓ Allowing well-behaved pets into the workplace (yup, they are family too!)

✓ Staying late after work to help employees work on Halloween costumes for their kids

✓ Researching eldercare alternatives for an employee who needed help with his parents (an increasing challenge for many "Boomers")

✓ Sending birthday cards or cakes to employees' family members

✓ Setting up special e-mail and resource areas on the company Intranet for employees' children

✓ Locating resources (the company lawyer) for an employee who was struggling with his health insurance company (the HMO)

Here is an example of really showing support:

When people ask me why I stayed at Ogilvy for 27 years, I tell them this story: When I was pregnant with my first child—he's now 24— I had trouble with my pregnancy and was sent home for bed rest. After two weeks I couldn't take it anymore and went back to work. The president of the agency called me and said, "I am not going to allow you to go back and forth on the subway." He just sent his car in the morning and took me home at night. At that time I became a life-time employee of Ogilvy.

—Shelly Lazarus, chairman and CEO,
Ogilvy & Mather Worldwide[3]

Get Creative

"We've never done that here." "The policies don't support that." "I'd be in hot water with my boss if I allowed that." These are common refrains among managers who don't know their real power or who are afraid to test the limits of the family-friendly (or unfriendly) rules. Sure there are constraints and policy guidelines in most organizations. And you have to play by those rules to some degree. But often it pays to get creative on behalf of your employees and their needs.

see QUESTION

There was no such thing as job sharing in this organization. We have a long history and cemented policies. After the birth of our children, another director and I decided to go to our boss and ask about the possibility of sharing one job. The job was high level and critical to the organization, so at first there was tremendous concern about even trying it. But our boss took a risk, ran the idea up the flagpole and gained approval for a six-month test period. That was twelve years ago and we have been sharing the job effectively ever since. The creativity and flexibility of our boss allowed us both to balance family and work. We are tremendously grateful and loyal employees.

—Manager, public utility

Job sharing is just one example of a creative solution to a challenging situation. Here are some other strategies and solutions that managers, in collaboration with their employees, have come up with. Which might work for you?

✓ If employees must travel on weekends, offer something in exchange, such as comp time during the week or allowing family members to travel with the employee.

✓ When your employees travel to areas where they have family or friends, allow them to spend extra time with those people at the beginning or end of the trip.

✓ If company policy absolutely prohibits bringing pets to work, consider a picnic in a park where those furry family members are welcome.

✓ Give your employees a "floating" day off per year to be used for a special occasion. Or suggest they go home early on their birthday or anniversary.

✓ Have a party for your team and their families. Invite the kids (or hire sitters for small ones) and go for pizza together.

✓ When an employee asks about working from home, really explore that possibility. What are the upsides? Downsides? Get creative about how that might work to benefit both the employee and your team.

TO DO ...

✓ Do your employees already have computers at home? Consider subsidizing just the Internet costs so that they can work from home on an as-needed basis. Since monthly costs for Internet use are now flat, the charges will be minimal for the productivity you'll get in return.

The best kind of creativity is collaborative. Remember to brainstorm a list of ideas *with your employees* and be continuously open to new and innovative ways to balance family and work. Tailor and customize your strategies to employees' needs.

BOTTOM LINE

Good employees leave family-unfriendly workplaces. Do some of these ideas seem extreme to you? We suggest talking to your company's recruiter about the options some employers are including in recruitment packages. If family-friendly means to you allowing your employees to accept an occasional personal phone call, it's time to upgrade your knowledge and find out what's going on around you. There are positive payoffs for your efforts, including increased loyalty, money saved and the competitive edge that a loyal, committed workforce will provide. Become a family-friendly manager and keep your talent on your team.

Chapter 7

GOALS

Expand Options

The only career path I saw was up ... and up was in short supply!

—A.J.

Do you get a knot in your stomach when a valued employee begins a conversation with one of these phrases?

- ✓ I'd like to talk to you about my career . . .
- ✓ I really want to understand what my career options are . . .
- ✓ I'm interested in talking about my next step . . .
- ✓ I don't understand why he got that promotion. I thought I . . .
- ✓ It's only through a step up that I feel appreciated . . .

Feel the knot? It's understandable. You value employees with superb skills who have mastered the current job and want more. They may get calls from recruiters. They want a chance to run the project. They're in your office, looking to you for a much-needed, much-deserved conversation about moving up in the organization. You want to keep them. And "up" is in short supply.

You may lose some of them. However, our 20 years of research reveals that not all those who *say* they want vertical moves will leave if they don't get them. But they *will* leave if they are not challenged, growing, and having new experiences.

Moving Forward Instead of Up

What if your employees began to think about other ways of moving? What if each move challenged and rewarded them? What if they could move forward instead of up?

Sometimes you can prevent turnover by helping your employees identify several career goals. If employees see that you can support several viable alternatives within the organization, they see a future for themselves within the realities of that organization.

Right Person, Right Place, Right Time

This phrase is one that human resource professionals and managers alike have sought to make work. It's never been easy. But here's a twist to consider: What if there were more right places? Would there not be more right times for all those right people?

We believe that there are five possible moves in addition to moving up. We also believe that the more specifically you can outline those moves, the less your talented employees will see *other* grass as greener. Consider talking with your employees about moves in several (or all!) of the following directions:

1. *Lateral Movement:* Moving across or horizontally
2. *Realignment:* Moving downward to open new opportunities
3. *Exploration:* Temporary moves intended for researching other options
4. *Enrichment:* Growing in place
5. *Relocation:* Moving to another organization

see CAREER

If you notice that four of these options (all but enrichment) raise the possibility of your talented people moving *away* from you, you're right. If this makes you nervous, you're in the majority. If you've spent time and resources building a strong, functioning team, you don't want to lose them to other managers and other parts of the organization. What's in it for you?

There may not be anything in it for you, except that the talent you have developed may *not* be lost to your organization! Your best people will leave if they feel that you are hoarding their talent, not exposing them to other managers and other departments within the organization who could use their talent.

The choice may be yours. The good news (if you choose not to hoard talent) is that your reputation as a manager who cares about development may draw other talented people who want to work on *your* team.

One of the authors once worked for a large corporation where she and her manager had a great relationship for many years. One day an opportunity surfaced that clearly would make even better use of her skills. Her manager, she later learned, lost a lot of sleep. Losing the employee meant losing a valuable asset to the team, but to encourage her move to a new start-up division would be a win for the employee and the organization. The manager bit the bullet, and a phenomenal opportunity resulted. The employee stayed with the organization for several productive years and her manager enjoyed a reputation as a strong people developer.

Lateral Movement

Until recently, lateral moves meant that your career might be headed for a dead end. Not today. Lateral moves offer much-needed breadth of experience. Taking a lateral move should mean applying current experience in a new job at the same level, but with different duties or challenges. Help employees see that lateral moves can improve skills or shift them from a slow-growing function to an expanding part of the organization. As you hold this discussion, be sure your people under-stand that you're not trying to get rid of them but to retain their talent for the organization.

TO DO . . .

Ask your employees:

- ✓ Which of your skills can be applied beyond your present job and present department?
- ✓ If you take a lateral move into a new area, what long-term career opportunities does it provide?
- ✓ What three skills are most transferable to another department?
- ✓ What other department interests you?

Enrichment

This might be the easiest option to discuss—but it's also one of the most ignored. Most folks seem to think they need to move out of their current position to develop. Never has this been less true. Most of your employees' work is changing constantly. Enrichment means that employees expand the job, refine their expertise, or find depth in areas they really enjoy. You can help.

Here's the critical question for you (and them) to ponder: What can employees do, or learn to do, that will energize their work and bring them closer to achieving their goals and the goals of the organization?

see ENRICH

I worked for a great boss as a project manager, but I knew (and she really knew too) that I could do more. I had fantastic artistic skills (if I do say so myself), and my boss did something about it. She sent me to graphic recording school and has used my new skills in her business. I am thrilled!

—Project manager

TO DO...

Try asking your employees:

✓ What are your goals?
✓ What do you enjoy most about your job?
✓ What could be added to your job to make it more satisfying?
✓ What internal and external training programs could you pursue to help enrich your job?

Exploration

It happens. We reach a stage in our careers when we aren't sure of what we want or what choices are available, or even what's appropriate. This one involves gathering information to decide if the grass is indeed greener elsewhere. Encourage your people to consider taking short-term job assignments in other parts of the organization, participating on project teams with people from other departments or even going on informational interviews. (These are interviews with people whose job your employee *thinks* he or she wants.)

see OPPORTUNITIES

Giving a talented person whose expertise you need the chance to explore other teams isn't easy. But people are less likely to feel trapped in their current jobs when they have other choices. They may find out that the grass isn't greener.

TO DO...

Consider asking your employees:

✓ What other areas of the company interest you?
✓ If you could start your career over, what would you do differently?
✓ Which of our current organization task forces interest you? Which might give you the best view of another part of this organization?

Realignment

In the old world of "up is the only way," the thought of moving downward would probably be the last on anyone's list of options. But sometimes the path to a career goal involves a step backward, to gain a better position for the next move.

Alas

An excellent technical contributor was promoted to manager. At first he liked the work. It still had some technical components and he managed other bright individual contributors. But over time he moved more and more into managing those bright others, searching for ways to bring more work to the unit, and fighting administrative battles. He felt he had made a mistake and longed to return to a technical position. He had outgrown his previous position but longed for something with the new hardware group. He went to his manager to admit his mistake and request a move. His manager resisted, suggesting he give it more time or that he enroll in a training course to improve his management skills. Instead, he applied for a job with a competitor that was precisely what he wanted.

This company lost a talented person because neither he nor his manager discussed realignment.

TO DO...

Try one of these with an employee:

✓ If you take an assignment in another area, what will be the opportunities for future growth and development?

✓ Are you willing to accept the same or a lower salary to make a fresh start in a new area?

✓ How will this new position enable you to use the skills you really enjoy?

Relocation

Why even mention relocation when we're talking about retention? Why not suggest that it means a move to another group within your own organization? Because it doesn't. Relocation means that you've thought about all the options and you realize that the best career step for this employee is to look elsewhere. This might happen when:

✓ An employee's skills, interests and values just don't fit his or her work
✓ An employee's career goals are all unrealistic for your organization
✓ An employee is committed to pursuing entrepreneurial interests
✓ An employee's technical skills are undervalued in the organization

So how is relocation a retention vehicle? Most employees who have had this kind of straight talk conversation with their own managers do move on. Often they end up being the best ambassadors for that organization after they leave!

Don't have the relocation conversation unless you and your employee have really searched your *internal* labor market.

TO DO . . .

Consider asking:

✓ Do you know people who have left this company and gone somewhere else? What were their experiences like? Can you talk with these individuals before deciding what to do?

✓ What is it about this company that's making you feel you want to look outside? How has the company changed?
✓ If you leave here, what are your long-term career opportunities in another organization?

When Up Is the Only Way

Sometimes, it just is. Yes, vertical advancement is the classic step up the corporate ladder. Your job is to identify and communicate what a talented employee's vertical options could include. Of course, advancement is most likely when an employee's abilities match the needs of the organization. You must interpret the organization's strategic direction to your team so that they select assignments that will prepare them for impending changes and openings. Clearly, technical excellence and political savvy are both critical to gaining that next step. Talented people need straight feedback and continual coaching to reach their vertical career goals.

TO DO . . .

Try asking your employees:

✓ Who is your competition for that next position? What are their strengths and weaknesses?
✓ How has your job performance been during the last year? How has it prepared you for the next step?
✓ Why should this company promote you?

BOTTOM LINE

Helping employees reach their goals often means helping them consider moves they may not have taken seriously before. Ask key questions to help them see what they could gain by trying a move that isn't a simple vertical step. You will increase your organization's chances of keeping the employee. And you will acquire a good reputation as a strategist and developer of people.

Chapter 8

HIRE

Fit is It

One thing that slowed me down for a while was when we hired in a hurry and didn't think about the fit between the new hires and the rest of the team. It ended up hurting everyone.

—A.J.

Get the right people in the door in the first place and you increase the odds of keeping them. As the manager, you have the clearest sense of the "right fit" for your department. Seems logical, doesn't it? Yet some managers see the selection process as a less important part of their jobs. They spend little time identifying the critical success factors for a position, preparing and conducting excellent interviews based on those factors and, finally, evaluating and comparing the candidates before making a hiring decision. They may even turn much of the hiring process over to Human Resources instead of being involved themselves. The hiring process and ultimate hiring decisions are, in fact, among the most important tasks you have as a manager—*and a critical retention strategy.*

What is Right Fit?

How do you know if a candidate will fit or not? How do you measure fit, manage your biases and make more objective hiring decisions? Here is a start.

Measuring Fit

By "right fit" we mean a person whose skills and interests match with the requirements of the job you are trying to fill. The right person's core values will be consistent with the values of the organization. You need to do your homework, be prepared and be clear about your wants and needs.

Southwest Airlines is an organization that looks for fit, especially with the company culture. A pilot told us about his own interview and selection process. He had heard that Southwest managers "hire for attitude and train for skill." The interviews they conducted with him certainly seemed to support that rumor. Through multiple interviews he realized that the interviewers seemed to care more about who he was as a person than the fact that he had a stellar aviation background that should have made him an obvious choice. They probed for attitudes, beliefs and behaviors that would give them clues about how he might treat flight attendants or peers, how he might deal with conflict at work, and what mattered most to him.

Southwest managers tested his sense of humor in many ways during the series of interviews, and it became clear to him that they were truly looking for a fit between the way work gets done at Southwest Airlines and his personality.

Why does Southwest care about an employee's sense of humor (especially the pilot's)? Because the ability and willingness to laugh and have fun on the job is highly valued in that organization. Southwest's values include providing "outrageous customer service" and having *fun* at work. To truly fit into their culture, employees need to be able to laugh (especially at themselves), enjoy work and provide a fun environment for those who report to them.

"Fit" also means alignment between the job requirements and the candidate's skills and interests. How often have you seen employees leave (on their own or with a push) because they simply did not have the right skills or interests? Why didn't the hiring manager see that coming? How can you avoid that expensive mistake?

TO DO . . .

✓ ***Analyze the job***, get input from others to clarify the tasks, traits and style required. Once you have identified these success factors, you can begin to create interview questions that will help you decide if the person actually has these skills or traits. (See the case study below.)

✓ ***Create an interview guide*** with your carefully prepared behavioral questions. (Read on for some examples.) Behavioral questions allow you to learn how candidates have handled certain situations in the past. Their answers will help you predict their ability to handle similar situations in the future. Use the same questions for all candidates so that you can later compare them.

✓ ***Include others*** in the interview process. Have potential team members, direct reports and peers of these future employees interview them (maybe asking different questions from yours) and give you their input. Several heads are definitely better than one when it comes to hiring.

✓ ***Consider using personality and skill assessments*** to assist you in making the decision. Get information from your Human Resources department about tools that might help you evaluate candidates' skills, work interests and even values. Note: Be certain that you do not make a hiring decision based on just one tool.

In Search of Fit

Joe, a manager in a high-tech company, has an opening for a supervisor in the marketing department. He has placed Internet and newspaper ads and now has a stack of resumes to consider. With help from his Human Resources representative, he has narrowed the field to the top ten candidates and is ready to interview. On paper all ten look like great fits for the job—technically.

Joe is pretty savvy and has hired many people. Some worked out great and some were absolute flops. All had looked good on paper. This time, though, Joe is prepared to get the *right fit!* He has identified the core values of his department. (Values can vary by department, division and team.) They include honesty and integrity, teamwork, customer focus and work/life balance.

He is clear about the most critical technical skills. The screening process has already weeded out those who don't have them. The critical leadership competencies for the role include motivating others, building a team, and dealing with ambiguity. Joe knows that the right fit will be a person with those skills. Next, Joe creates his interview guide with the questions he thinks can help him identify the relevant abilities, interests and values of his candidates. Here are three questions on Joe's sheet:

1. Tell me about a work incident when you were totally honest, despite a potential risk or downside for the honesty.
2. How did you handle a recent situation where the direction from above was unclear and circumstances were changing?
3. Describe how you motivated a group of people to do something they did not want to do.

These questions may seem tough to answer, and they are. Joe allows time for the candidates to ponder the question and he eases the tension by suggesting they take their time or by acknowledging it's a tough question. You can imagine that each of these questions leads Joe and his candidates into potentially deep discussions that could reveal where each candidate truly lines up on the value or leadership competency at hand. The questions are open-ended, not yes or no. They are not leading, as in, "Do you value work/life balance?" They are behavioral, causing the candidates to search their memories for real-life examples.

Joe takes a few notes as the interviews progress so that he will not forget some of the more critical answers they give or assumptions he

see VALUES

makes along the way. He probes to learn more about each topic until he feels he truly knows where all the candidates line up on these critical success factors. Of course he asks questions to validate their technical expertise as well.

After the interviews, Joe compares notes with his other interviewers. He also looks at the assessment results that come to him from Human Resources to see if he needs to call any candidates in for follow-up interviews to explore any red-flag areas.

Joe compares his candidates by scoring them on a 1–5 scale on each of his critical success factors that he had identified for the job. They include:

✓ Technical skills
✓ Leadership competencies
✓ Values

As he scores them he reviews his notes and thinks about:

✓ The level of each candidate's sincerity
✓ Expressed enthusiasm and interest in the work
✓ Probable level of skill

He gives a 5 to those who seem to possess this skill, trait or value to a very high degree and a 1 to those who appear not to have it.

While there is no such thing as a totally objective interview or selection process, this method allows Joe to make the most objective decision possible. He proceeds to offer the job to the candidate whom he feels meets the right-fit criteria the best.

By the way, had none of the candidates measured up to the criteria Joe set, he was willing to start over with a new batch of candidates. He had learned from past mistakes that it was too costly to choose wrong and that it was worth the wait for the right fit!

They Are Choosing Too

A much sought-after new hire, when explaining why a company was selected: "They put me first. They asked what do you want to do, what are your ideas, and so on."

Be aware that your talented candidates are walking in that interview door well prepared and typically with multiple career or job choices available to them. Imagine that they arrive with a grid in their heads (or sometimes on paper). That grid might look like this:

My wants/needs (candidate)	Your organization	Your competitor	Another job
Compensation			
Perks			
Team			
Geography			
Training			
Creativity			
Vacation			

This grid helps the candidate ask you questions and evaluate the opportunity somewhat objectively (and compare yours to other job opportunities).

Be prepared to *sell* your organization or team to candidates by addressing the key issues they raise. Think carefully about what you and your team can offer to candidates and be ready to give specific examples. For example, if you are offering a great team environment and camaraderie, demonstrate that by having all team members meet and briefly interview your top candidates. Think about your team or organizational "wow" factors—those things that differentiate you from the rest. It might be your cutting edge technology, your highly creative environment or the atmosphere of fun that permeates the workplace. Whatever your unique selling proposition is, recognize it and leverage it during the interview. Note: Remember—don't oversell. Painting a too-rosy picture can backfire if your new recruits find out that you were exaggerating.

A high-technology company recognized after several years of unsuccessful recruiting that it was simply not selling its organization. The recruiters and managers knew how terrific the culture was and that the technology was the best in the business—but they just had not tooted their horn sufficiently. Once they began to spend more time in the interviews demonstrating their cutting-edge products, their success rate skyrocketed and they began to successfully grab the best of the best high-tech talent. They have now tripled the time they used to spend demonstrating products during key interviews.

TO DO . . .

✓ Remember to sell talented prospects on your organization. Think about what makes your company unique and a great place to work.
✓ Place a copy of this book on your desk during the interview. (Candidates will get the hint that keeping good people is important to you.) To go a step further, show them the book and ask them which of the chapters (A–Z) are most relevant to retaining *them*.

Who, Me? Biased?

What if "right fit" means *like me* or *the right age* or *shape/size* or *gender* or *color?* It doesn't—or shouldn't. The right fit excuse has been used many times to put clones (usually clones of the boss) in jobs. That is certainly not what we mean by "right fit." In fact, if you spend the time to identify those critical factors that spell success for a particular job and then select people against those criteria, you will be most apt to avoid dismissing potentially wonderful candidates.

We all have biases and we often make assumptions based on them. Let's test some of your assumptions about getting the right person in the job. Ask yourself as you read this sample assumption list, "Have I ever thought this about a person or a job?" Be brutally honest—you don't have to tell anyone how you responded!

Assumption Testing

Assumption: Single mothers will be a risk because when their children are ill, they will not show up.

Fact: Some single moms so need this job that they will find a way to make it to work! Some have excellent contingency planning skills and have two or three backup tactics to rely on when the kids are sick. (And remember—it is illegal to ask if they are a single mom or have children.)

Assumption: A seriously overweight person can't do this job because of the air travel required.

Fact: Overweight or obese individuals certainly can find ways of doing the job, even if it demands air travel. And remember, obesity is viewed by law as a disability and therefore protected by the ADA (Americans with Disabilities Act). That means that you must consider accommodation for a candidate who is qualified to do the work.

Assumption: He is _____ (fill in the ethnicity) and therefore won't be the go-getter we need.

Fact: Ethnicity has no correlation to work traits or motivation, such as being a go-getter, or having the desire to go the extra mile.

Assumption: She has never done this exact job before so would be a huge hiring risk.

Fact: While we often look for folks who have done the job before, there are certainly other criteria to consider when assessing candidates. For example, have they seen it done (good and bad situations), can they describe (do they know) how it is done, and are they agile learners? Some who have done the job before are bored with it and may not have the same interest level as someone newer to the task. Also, if everything else lines up (such as values, traits and interests) you might want to choose the candidate for whom this is new or a stretch, especially if the missing skills are readily trainable.

Assumption: He is too old/too young for this job.

Fact: What's age got to do with it? The famous heart surgeon Michael Debakey is now 90 years old and still considered the best of the best in his specialty. A younger than the norm or older than the norm person may in fact have some additional barriers to overcome in a particular industry, company or job—but we all have barriers of one kind or another.

Assumption: We need a man in this job because it is too emotionally challenging for a woman.

Fact: Some women might handle the emotionally charged environment even more effectively than a man. The ability to function well is made up of a combination of traits, skills, behaviors and experience that is *gender neutral* (meaning gender does not predict ability).

When you find yourself forming assumptions about candidates based on their gender or size or color (and by the way, we all do that sometimes), then gently move yourself back to the key criteria you have identified and your methodology for assessing all of your candidates fairly. Check out your biases, test your assumptions and then select for the right fit.

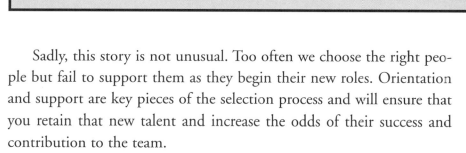

Alas

A manufacturing organization was growing and hired six new supervisors and managers to fill key roles in its new plants. The selection process was beautifully handled and included assessments, multiple interviewers and competency-based, thorough interviews. The right people were hired and the entire organization heaved a sigh of relief. Thank goodness that was over! Everyone went back to work and the new hires were basically sent to their new job to figure it out. Within six months one of the new stars had taken another job, stating in the exit interview that he received no mentoring or assistance as he took on the new tasks—it was just too frustrating, and he was not used to feeling like a failure. Two others were being critically reviewed as not having the "right stuff" after all. The remaining three were stumbling along trying to figure it out on their own. Meanwhile, the teams that reported to these folks were frustrated and less than impressed with these new heroes—they certainly did not seem to live up to the expectations everyone had of them.

Sadly, this story is not unusual. Too often we choose the right people but fail to support them as they begin their new roles. Orientation and support are key pieces of the selection process and will ensure that you retain that new talent and increase the odds of their success and contribution to the team.

Isn't orientation something the Human Resources department handles? Maybe so—for teaching about the overall company policies and procedures. But you, the manager, get to do the rest. Better yet, involve your team in the process.

TO DO . . .

✓ Have an "expectations exchange" with your new employees. Clearly define what you expect from them and ask what they are expecting from you and the team.

✓ Spend time teaching them about the organization they have just joined. Tell stories, share your experiences and knowledge about the culture and history.

✓ Involve your key people in the new hires' orientation. Expose new employees to others' views and stories as well as your own.

✓ Mentor and find mentors for them as they work to close the inevitable skill gaps (you no doubt identified those in the interview process).

✓ Be available to support them in this uncertain early stage of their employment. That may mean seeking them out to see how they are doing, asking about the commute and the family's adjustment to the move, and creating the sense that you are behind them all the way and invested in their success and happiness in their new job.

Re-Recruit As Well

A successful accountant, tragically hit by a bus and killed, arrives at the Pearly Gates and is welcomed by St. Peter, who says that she will need to spend one day in Heaven and one day in Hell before she decides where she would like to spend eternity. With great trepidation she enters Hell and is amazed to find a beautiful golf course, friends and colleagues who welcome her, terrific food, a great party and even a nice-guy devil. At the end of her day, she regretfully leaves Hell in order to experience her day in Heaven. That experience is quite good also, with the clouds, angels, harps and singing that she expected.

St. Peter pushes her to make the decision of a lifetime (and beyond). In which place would she spend eternity—Heaven or Hell? You guessed it, she chooses Hell. When she returns to Hell she finds a desolate wasteland and her friends dressed in rags and picking up garbage. There are no parties—only misery and despair. She says to the Devil, "I don't understand, yesterday I was here and there was a golf course and a country club, and we ate lobster and we danced and had a great time. Now I see a wasteland and all my friends look miserable." The Devil looks at her and smiles. "Yesterday we were recruiting you; today you're an employee."

If you chuckled knowingly at this story, it may be because there is a shred (or more) of truth to it. You may have experienced it yourself—the wining and dining during the recruitment phase (it's almost like courting) and then a cold, cruel reality once you signed on. If cold reality strikes too soon, you will surely lose that new gem. Research shows that you actually re-recruit your new hires for the first three years in which they are on board and that they are easily enticed away during that time.

But what about the rest of your talent? While you are busy hiring the best-fit candidates for key roles on your team, do a little re-recruiting along the way. Often candidates and new employees are viewed as close to perfect (their warts haven't surfaced yet) and they get all the attention. If you have done a great job of selecting, you will have a whole new stable of stars. Your long-term employees can feel less noticed, less appreciated and perhaps even taken for granted as you carefully select, orient and train these new folks. Avoid that dangerous phenomenon by re-recruiting your talent. Show your current employees that they are important and critical to you and to the success of your team, especially as you recruit new team members.

BOTTOM LINE

Fit is it when it comes to hiring. If you get the right people in the right roles in your organization and on your team, you will absolutely increase the odds of retaining them.

Chapter 9

INFORMATION

Share It

I felt like I was never really a part of the organization . . . I mean,
I often read about what we were doing in the news!

—A.J.

So what's the big deal about information? In this busy, time-crunched environment, you simply may not have time to share information with your employees. What if you don't?

First: It's hard for you to do your best without information. The same is true for your employees.

Second: You will lose your talent—maybe not today, but eventually those with choices will leave you.

Having The Scoop or Out of the Loop

Information is power. But you've known that for a long time. As kids we knew that having the inside scoop is *cool* and we felt important if we were given information that others did not have. If information is power, then being out of the loop—lacking information—might leave one powerless. Research[1] shows that people want a boss with influence and power in the organization. Think about your own work experience and you will probably agree that you would much rather work for someone who is in the loop than a boss who is clueless and has no chance of being clued in. Your employees are no different. They want you to be in the loop and they want and need you to bring them in too.

In The Absence of Information They Will Make it Up

Information sharing during times of dramatic change is even more critical than during stable times. We have seen dozens of examples of organizations going through major change where high level managers decided to withhold information (we acknowledge that at times you simply *cannot* share) and where middle managers hoarded information out of fear of losing their power or importance.

Check out what might happen when you withhold information about change:

Senior Manager Thinks	Employees Think
It's too early to tell them.	Silence must mean it's pretty bad.
This news is too frightening— we'd better wait.	They're moving the company to Panama.
I'm afraid if we tell them, productivity will drop.	The company's going belly-up. Where else can I get a job?

Notice that the manager is trying to protect the employees and prevent all the water cooler talk that can put a huge dent in work productivity. Ironically, the silence and protection backfires. What do you suppose happens to productivity as these employees worry about their jobs and update their resumes?

In contrast, where top leaders give information as early and honestly as possible and hold managers accountable for passing the news down, employees actually feel important and valued and the productivity dip is minimized.

Another good reason to share information is that your employees might be able to help. A good example of this occurred at Beth Israel Hospital.

The hospital had a policy of never eliminating positions through layoffs—a commitment it had kept its entire history, including when it merged with another hospital. Several years ago the policy was tested when the hospital faced a potential $20 million deficit. Management shared the news with the staff and asked for its help. Within 10 days it received 4,000 cost-saving ideas from employees. Sixteen task forces were formed to deal with them. While most of the strategies involved tighter controls on purchasing, employees also suggested forgoing raises and holding off on accrued paid time off. By the end of the year, enough savings had been realized to eliminate the need for layoffs.[2] Similar stories from other major organizations demonstrate the viability of information sharing for the purpose of problem solving.

Getting Your Fair Share

So how do you know what and how much to share? The answer is, it depends. It depends primarily on your organization's culture and the philosophy of your upper management. At one end of the openness continuum lies the philosophy of Jack Stack, president and CEO of Springfield Remanufacturing Company (SRC) in Springfield, Missouri. He wrote *The Great Game of Business*, and espouses "open book management," a philosophy and set of beliefs and business practices that have been adopted by dozens of highly successful organizations. He says, "We are building a company in which everyone tells the truth every day—not because everyone is honest, but because everyone has access to the same information: operating metrics, financial data, valuation estimates. The more people understand what's really going on in their company, the more eager they are to help solve its problems."[3] It's clear that when Jack Stack says open book, he means *open book*—tell it all!

You may not work in such an information-open environment. Consider the consequences of your communication style and the culture in which you manage. Do what you can to share as much as you can with your employees. The result will be increased commitment and enhanced odds of keeping your best people.

No—You Don't Need a Crystal Ball

see CAREER

As a manager in the new millenium, you are expected to help your team look to the future. A key part of this role entails providing information that supports your employees' development and career advancement. You will need to look ahead, forecast what is coming around the bend, from your point of view. Share what you know about:

1. Your organization's strategic direction
2. Your profession, industry and organization's future
3. The emerging trends and new developments that may affect career possibilities
4. The cultural and political realities of your organization

As you forecast, your team members will better understand the changing world of work; they will learn to look broadly at their profession, industry and organization and see the trends and implications in each. They will also feel more competent and confident in their future marketability.

TO DO . . .

✓ Cut out articles that relate to your industry for your employees to read. You probably have access to industry-based newsletters, reports and magazines that other employees may never see. By distributing articles about events that are happening within your industry, you share critical information that can help them make decisions about their career development and advancement.

Have you ever had a boss tell you, "I knew that weeks ago, but couldn't (or decided not to) share it with you?" Isn't that infuriating? You may have thought: "Thanks a lot. A lot of good this does me now!" or "See if I trust you in the future," or "Why even tell me you knew? Is this a power trip?"

A CEO accepted the resignation of a member of his senior team and knew there would be an impact on the organization. When we asked him when he planned to share that information with his key players he responded, "I don't want to upset them during a tense time, so I think I'll wait until our staff meeting in two days."

What do you think? Good idea? No, bad idea. What are the odds that people won't find out about the resignation within the same day? People knew within the hour and were frustrated, disappointed and even angry that the CEO had not immediately informed them. Many felt distrusted, even undervalued by their boss as a result of his nondisclosure.

So, as a manager, when should you share information? *The sooner the better!* When you are clear about *what* you want or need to share, find a way to do it soon, especially if the information is about a major change that has a direct impact on people.

How To Share

Remember that the primary *why* in this book is to keep your talented employees. Volumes have been written about how to communicate with employees, both in normal times and during times of dramatic change. Face-to-face, video, newsletter, e-mail, voice mail, open forums and bulletin boards all have their place in effectively communicating. The question is really which approach works best given your organization's culture and the message you are trying to send?

Here are a few guidelines as you ponder your communication choices.

TO DO . . .

✓ *Share information face to face*, especially if it is difficult to deliver or will affect your employees in significant ways. Tell your direct reports the news yourself, rather than having them learn it via memo or from some other source. Let your supervisors give the news to their direct reports also. Research shows that people believe it and react more favorably when the news is delivered in this manner.

✓ *Beware of critical information flowing down* through many layers. If it must flow down, double-check to be sure the message is getting through. We all know what happens to a story when it has been repeated several times—it barely resembles the original.

✓ *Get creative.* The more creatively a message is sent, the greater the chance it will be noticed. Consider doing the unexpected. If people are used to hearing news via a memo, try face-to-face or video next time.

Close to the Vest?

Building an information-rich culture can be challenging. After all, there will be times when you are privy to information that you simply cannot share with your employees. Here are a few simple guidelines to help ensure that you handle the situation appropriately but without alienating your employees. When the information must be held in confidence:

✓ Don't share no matter how tempting the information might be.

✓ Never use information-withholding as a power tool. If you are given proprietary or "secret" information, do not tell people you have it unless they ask you.

✓ If people ask you if you have information, be honest. Don't tell them you don't have information if you do.

✓ Tell them that you are not at liberty to share and tell them why, for example, "The information is sensitive or proprietary" or "I have been asked to keep it confidential and I need to honor that request."

✓ Be prepared for the possibility that your responses may not please people and some may feel that you really should or could tell them if you wanted to. If you establish a track record of early, honest information sharing, you will have more room to occasionally withhold information when the situation dictates.

I guess our greatest technique and our greatest accomplishment is this commitment to communicating with them [Wal-Mart employees] in every way that we possibly can, and listening to them constantly. . . . You've got to put their interest first, and eventually it will come back to the company.

— Sam Walton, Wal-Mart founder[4]

It's A Two-Way Street

So far we have focused on the sharing of information and of communicating early and honestly. Getting information is also a way of keeping your employees. People want to be heard. They want to have input regarding their jobs, the work at hand and the goals and strategies of the team and organization. As a manager, you need to ask for that input.

While most employees are expected to come to their managers if there is a problem, often they don't because they don't feel comfortable or because the manager doesn't offer the opportunity. As a manager you must make sure your employees feel comfortable talking to you. Set aside time just for this purpose by scheduling regular meetings or casual weekly breakfasts or lunches with your group.[5]

How important is two-way communication? Consider this story:

Alas

It was 3:00 A.M. in the South China Sea on June 3, 1969, when the USS Frank E. Evans was cut in half by the HMAS Melbourne (an Australian aircraft carrier) after inexplicably turning in front of it. The forward half of the Evans sank in three minutes. The commanding officer woke up in the water and many of the seamen aboard the ship perished.

Lt. Rodger Ramsey's night orders from the commander were specifically to awaken him if the Evans changed its course, but Ramsey never did. Reports stated that he was afraid to make the call. As a result, many of the Lieutenant's fellow shipmates died, the ship itself suffered severe damage and the career of Commander Albert S. McLemore was over.

All because an "employee" didn't feel safe enough to communicate vital information to "management."[6]

Poor communication may seldom yield such dire consequences. But there are almost always measurable costs.

BOTTOM LINE

Stay in the loop. Keep your employees in the loop. It will help you keep your talent.

Chapter 10

Jerk

Don't Be One

I know one department that kept losing talented people, one after the other. It was no mystery really. The manager was a complete jerk.

—A.J.

Warning: If this book landed on your desk with a bookmark here, pay attention!

People cautioned us not to write this chapter, or at least not to use this title. But to avoid this topic is to avoid discussing a primary reason that people leave their jobs. Employees will leave if they don't like their boss even when they are well paid, receive recognition and have a chance to learn and grow. In fact, disliking the boss is one of the top causes of talent loss. Take a look at this exit interview:

Interviewer:	Mathew, why have you decided to leave the organization? I know that we pay competitively and you just received a bonus.
Mathew:	Is this confidential?
Interviewer:	Definitely, yes.

Mathew: The pay is fine. The work is fine. But my boss is impossible. He is so difficult to work with and I've decided life is too short to spend it working for a jerk.

Have you ever worked for a jerk? Any jerks in your organization? This chapter is not about labeling people as jerks and letting the rest of us off the hook. It is about defining jerk-like behaviors and the "jerk mode" that people occasionally assume. It is about learning to assess whether or not you exhibit those behaviors and how often. And it's about trying to change for the better. Why? To keep your talented people.

Alas

Five years ago my father died on a business day, during which most executive-level management from my firm were out of state for a seminar. I was told, by telephone, that there was no reason for me to go home because my father was already dead. I was also told it was unreasonable for me to take more than a few hours off to attend the funeral. A few months later the CEO himself informed me that despite my 17 years of excellent performance, loyalty and upward mobility in the company, I was being passed over for promotion because I hadn't gotten over my grief soon enough. He told me that grieving for more than a week was excessive and unhealthy, and he had been concerned that I had taken three days off after my father's death. Moreover, he stated that I was too emotionally attached to my family and if I wanted a career with his firm, I would have to "loosen" my family ties. When the opportunity to leave his company presented itself, this incident was a major factor in my decision.

—Letter to the Editor, *Newsweek*, February 8, 1999, p.16

Fortunately, most people in jerk mode are not this brutal. The behaviors that characterize a jerk range from mild to severe in their negative impact on employees.

What Is a Jerk?

We asked dozens of people, "What do jerks act like or look like?" This checklist reflects what we heard. Do you dare to score yourself?

Behavior Checklist

Instructions: Score yourself on the following behaviors, using a 0–5 scale: zero means you never act this way and five means you often act this way.

	0–5
Intimidate	_____
Condescend or demean	_____
Act arrogant	_____
Withhold praise	_____
Slam doors, pound the table when angry	_____
Swear	_____
Behave rudely	_____
Belittle people in front of others	_____
Micro-manage	_____
Manage up, not down	_____
Always look out for number one	_____
Give only negative feedback	_____
Yell at people	_____
Lie	_____
Act above the rules	_____
Enjoy making people sweat	_____
Act superior/smarter than everyone else	_____
Show disrespect	_____
Act sexist	_____
Act racist	_____
Withhold critical information	_____
Use inappropriate humor	_____
Blow up in meetings	_____
Start every sentence with "I"	_____
Steal credit or the spotlight from others	_____

Block career moves (prevent promotion or
    hold onto "stars") _____

Distrust everyone _____

Show favoritism _____

Humiliate and embarrass others _____

Criticize constantly (often at a personal level) _____

Overuse sarcasm _____

Deliberately ignore or isolate some people _____

Set impossible goals or deadlines _____

Never accept blame, let others take the hit _____

Undermine authority _____

Show lack of caring for people _____

Betray trust or confidences _____

Gossip/spread rumors _____

Act as if others are stupid _____

Have "sloppy moods" (when feeling down,
    take it out on others) _____

Use fear as a motivator _____

Show revenge _____

Total score: _____

Note: This assessment is an insight tool, not a validated instrument. The following interpretation guidelines are just that—guidelines.

Interpretation Guidelines

(0–20) Although you have a bad day now and then, you are probably not viewed as a jerk. Watch those behaviors where you scored above a three and get more feedback from your employees.

(20–60) Look out! You could be viewed as a jerk by some, at least in some situations. Commit to reading and implementing two or more chapters in this book.

(60 or more) You are at high risk for losing talent. Get more feedback and consider getting a coach.

If you checked none of the behaviors on this assessment, you're either a saint or you have a few blind spots. In other words, most of us do exhibit some of these behaviors some of the time. The question is how many and how often? And what effect is your behavior having on the people who report to you?

Who, Me?

We are all jerks sometimes. From time to time you might exhibit jerk-like behaviors or move into jerk mode. Some of us do it when we feel backed into a corner, stressed out or when someone pushes the wrong buttons. For others, these ineffective behaviors have simply become habit. Whatever the reason, are they negative or frequent enough to inhibit your effectiveness as a manager? How do your employees really view you and how does it affect their job satisfaction? How many of them are considering leaving you for a better boss?

Give your results from the jerk checklist some serious thought. Ask your friends at work to look at the list with you and give you honest feedback. (If you don't have any friends, that may be a clue.) Ask family members to give you insight as well. If others agree that you *often* exhibit more than one or two of those behaviors, you are at high risk for losing talent. Jerk-like behaviors are so damaging that even one or two can negate all of your other strengths as a boss.

I had no idea that my employees viewed me as such a jerk. We had 360-degree feedback [input from boss, peers, subordinates, even customers] as a part of a leadership development program. Employees had a chance to type in comments at the end of a lengthy computerized survey. My employees basically told me that I came across as insensitive and uncaring. They said that my drive to get results seemed to be at any cost, including employee health and morale. I was so shocked at this feedback. I felt terrible. Now I'm working with a coach to help me figure out how to change my behaviors. The first step was finding out how my employees viewed me.

—Senior manager, engineering firm

see TRUTH

see DIGNITY

If you have never had an in-depth *360-degree feedback assessment*, you may want to consider it. The feedback should come to you anonymously, and it should be used for your own awareness and development. Recognizing your ineffective and potentially damaging behaviors is the first step to doing something about them.

Sadly, too many corporate American heroes operate in jerk mode too much of the time. Some have temper tantrums in staff meetings, even throw things. Others embarrass and humiliate people openly and frequently. Because of their status, some of these leaders have been allowed to behave as jerks and seem to have gotten away with it. You may have worked for one of these people.

If it worked for them, why not for you? Because you will be more effective if your employees like and respect you. People respond when they are treated with dignity. They work harder for bosses they like. With competition for good people increasing, it is critical that you keep your stars and be able to recruit new talent when necessary. Jerks will be unable to do either as their reputations spread.

Once a Jerk, Always a Jerk?

Just as you can learn new leadership skills at any age, you can stop ineffective behaviors or replace them with more effective ones.

I used to blow up at people. When I was under stress and someone said the wrong thing, I just lost control. I yelled, turned red in the face and pounded the table. The result was that people used to tiptoe around me. They hid bad news and took few risks, fearing my temper if they failed. People were intimidated. We lost creativity, productivity and some talent along the way. All because of my uncontrolled temper.

Now I'm better, at least 90 percent of the time. It took some time and a lot of effort, but I now have a handle on my emotions. When I feel the blood pressure rise and my anger coming on, I picture a stop sign. I stop, take three slow, deep breaths and then we talk about the problem. What a difference—both in how I feel about myself and how my employees react.

—Manager, marketing and sales department

Because behaviors are learned, we know that it is possible to change. It may not be easy, but it is possible. The difficulty of changing ineffective behaviors depends on the answers to several questions:

✓ How ingrained is the behavior? Have you been acting this way for fifty years, or for three? Some of those long-term habits are certainly more difficult to break than those more recently learned.

✓ Are you crystal clear about what the desired behavior will look like? A clear picture of the goal will certainly make it easier to get there.

✓ Do you have resources available to help you? It's easier to change if you have people supporting you.

✓ How complex is the behavior? You may be able to simply decide to stop telling off-color jokes and never do it again. Negative reactions under stress are more complicated and interwoven, so they will probably require more focus, more resources and a longer time to change. You may need to develop a new repertoire of behaviors from which to choose.

✓ *Do you really want to change? Why? If you can't answer this question, you will not change. You gotta want to.*

Once you decide to change, you can create your action plan.

TO DO . . .

✓ Get honest feedback somehow. You need a clear picture of how you look to others.

✓ Ask, "So what?" Think about the implications of your behaviors. Are they getting in the way of your effectiveness? Causing good people to leave?

✓ Take a stress management course.

✓ Exercise. Eat well. Sleep more. You choose.

✓ Try Tai Chi, Yoga, meditation or prayer.

✓ If you decide to change, seek help from others.

- Get a coach.
- Seek counseling.
- Attend a personal growth seminar.
- Read self-improvement books.
- Ask people to monitor and give you feedback as you attempt to change.

BOTTOM LINE

If you believe (or find out) that you often exhibit jerk-like behaviors, decide to change. This book exists to help you do it. Changing jerk-like behaviors may be the most important action you can take to keep your talent on your team.

Chapter 11

 **KICKS**

Get Some

My boss held the "all work, no play" philosophy. Work was simply not the place for fun.

—A.J.

What's your philosophy about fun at work? Do you believe in it? Have it? Support it? Make it happen? Discourage it? Check out your own beliefs and assumptions about fun at work. Then consider the possibility of *creating and supporting* kicks in the workplace as one way to keep your best people.

Research shows that a workplace that is seen as fun-loving generates enthusiasm. Enthusiasm leads to increased productivity, better customer service, a positive attitude about the company and significantly higher odds that your talent will stay. Most people want to have some light moments on the job. A dry, humorless, too serious workplace could send your talent searching for a better place to spend the majority of their waking hours.

If I were to redo my career, I would encourage more kicks.
—Retired vice president, engineering firm

Fun for One—Fun for All?

When was the last time you had a good laugh at work?

✓ Last year
✓ Last month
✓ Last week
✓ Yesterday

If your answer was yesterday, you're probably smiling as you read this.

When we think about having fun at work we realize that one person's fun can be another person's turn-off. We do not all view humor in the same way. If you doubt this, compare British and American comedies. Joke telling may be fun for you and ridiculous (or even insulting) to someone else. Some people get kicks out of decorating your office as a birthday surprise while others love to take a break to debate some current hot topic or to surf the Web. So as you think about the enjoyable workplace that you have the power to shape, remember to ask people what would make work more fun.

Fun-Free Zone

Unfortunately, the workplace is a fun-free zone in many organizations. In one study, workers graded their bosses on the degree to which they supported or allowed fun at work. The average grade was a measly C+.[1] If you're one of those C+ bosses and you are not having or allowing fun at work, why is that? Maybe you just were not raised that way. The bosses you learned from may have been fun-averse, serious taskmasters. Perhaps you believe that allowing frivolity or fun at work will cause you to lose control over your employees or fail to achieve results. You might think that moments of levity will set bad precedents and the group will never get back to business. Some of your concerns may be based on *fun myths*, beliefs and assumptions about having kicks in the workplace.

TO DO . . .

Check which of these myths you tend to believe in:

✓ Myth #1: Professionalism and fun are incompatible.
✓ Myth #2: You need toys and money to have fun.
✓ Myth #3: Fun means laughter.
✓ Myth #4: You have to plan for fun.
✓ Myth #5: Fun time at work will compromise our results.
✓ Myth #6: You have to have a good sense of humor (or be funny) to
            create a fun work environment.

Myth Debunking

These myths are just that—myths. Let's debunk them.

Myth #1: Professionalism and Fun Are Incompatible

Can you have fun and still maintain a professional work environment? It depends on the kind of fun you are talking about. Slapstick silliness (pie-in-the-face humor) will not fit well in a business-suit environment. But there are many appropriate ways to get some kicks in even the most buttoned-up workplace.

Every month we had client reports that were due and most us of dreaded the solitary extra-hours work that the task required. So we started a new tradition where we all planned to stay late one night each month. We went to a deli for snacks and good wine and then held a work party. Everyone was on their computer in their own office, but we took regular breaks, helped each other, enjoyed our food and wine together and had some laughs in the after-work

casual environment. It not only made the monthly task much more enjoyable, but it provided a type of team building for all of us.
—Consultant, management consulting firm

In another highly professional work environment, when someone is late to a meeting, they either have to sing a song or tell a new joke (in good taste!). People are on time more often since the new rule, but there is also a guaranteed chuckle as people slide in the door a minute or two late.

Most concern about having fun in a serious workplace is actually concern about inappropriate humor, loud behavior or poor timing. If employees' timing is off or their behavior is embarrassing or disruptive, you can give them that feedback, just as you would about any other of their work behaviors.

Myth #2: It Takes Toys and Money to Have Fun at Work

This is the sister myth to "It takes toys and money to have fun in life." When we asked dozens of people to reflect on fun times they remembered having at work, here is what we heard. (Notice how many of these examples cost money or involve toys.)

✓ "No specific time. It was just the day-to-day laughter my colleagues and I shared—mostly about small things."
✓ "We decorated my boss's office for his birthday. We used five bags of confetti from the shredding machine."
✓ "Spontaneous after-work trips to the local pizza parlor."
✓ "Verbal sparring with my brainy, funny colleagues."
✓ "When we had a huge project, a tight deadline and we had to work all night. I wouldn't want to do that often, but we had a good time, laughs in the middle of the night and a thrill when we finished the project."
✓ "Receiving this poem from my dedicated, funny employees whom I sent to Detroit on business: Roses are red, violets are blue, it's 30 below and we hate you."
✓ "In the midst of a big stressful project, our boss took us to a local park for a volleyball game during lunch. We still talk about it."

Toys and money certainly can help you have fun too. Microsoft and Amgen are two large companies with *fun* budgets. In both companies people are expected to work hard and play hard. Their play includes the occasional extravagant party or boat trip. While employees seem to greatly appreciate being treated to elaborate outings, most report that it is the day-to-day work environment that matters most to them. It has to be enjoyable.

Myth #3: Fun Means Laughter

Fun often does involve laughter or smiles. Sometimes people just need to take themselves less seriously.

We have to be so intellectual most of the time. We like to occasionally go off into silliness.

—Math professor and her tutors

But people can have fun at work without laughing or getting silly. An intriguing project and collaboration with wonderful teammates can truly be fun. Work that is meaningful and making a difference can be fun. Building something new can be fun.

Some of the most fun I ever had was in the early days of creating a completely new form of airplane. We were building something new that would make a difference. It was difficult and challenging but so much fun.

—Retired aeronautical engineer

Myth #4: You Have to Plan for Fun

Planned fun makes sense sometimes. The employee softball team provides fun and requires planning, as does an occasional employee picnic or the annual holiday party. But a lot of fun in the workplace just happens. It is spontaneous and unplanned.

We had been working so hard and had nailed all of our goals for the quarter. My boss called us into his office and presented the team with movie tickets—for the two o'clock show, that day! It was great. We took off as a group and felt like kids, playing hooky from school. It was so spontaneous and so appreciated.

—City government employee

Unplanned fun can be as simple as showing up at the staff meeting with muffins for everyone, asking a group of employees to join you for lunch at a new restaurant or taking an unplanned coffee break to just sit and talk about families or hobbies.

Myth #5: Fun Time at Work Will Compromise Results

This is one of the largest concerns of managers. Somehow many of them feel that every minute spent chuckling is a minute lost toward bottom-line results.

Alas

Somehow three of us stepped out of our offices at the same time, met in the hallway and began chatting. I don't even remember what we began laughing about but all three of us were really laughing (not very quietly). Our boss stepped out of his office with a furious, red-faced look and said, "Is this what I'm paying you for?" We were embarrassed, humiliated and angry. I left the company shortly after that, as did the other two people. It was a stifling environment where fun was not allowed. Ten years later, I still remember that incident.

—Retail sales manager

Research verifies that fun-loving environments are actually more productive than their humorless counterparts. A break, complete with laughter, can reenergize your employees and ready them for the next concentrated effort. In one Microsoft group, employees take breaks whenever they want to by surfing the Web or playing games on their computers. They say that these playful activities clear their minds so that when they return to the project at hand they are fresher and sharper.

You might be thinking, "If I allow my employees to surf the Web during work, they will never get their work done." Maybe you believe that only exceptional employees can be trusted to that degree. The secret to allowing fun at work is to be *crystal clear* with your employees about their performance goals. Cocreate those goals with them and make the goals measurable and specific.

Some of the most productive, successful organizations in the world are renowned for fun. Southwest Airlines CEO Herb Kelleher sets the famous Southwest tone. He has loaded baggage on Thanksgiving Day, ridden his Harley Davidson motorcycle into company headquarters and golfed at the Southwest golf tournament with just one club. He even arm-wrestled another CEO for the rights to an advertising slogan. Southwest flight attendants get their kicks by singing the departure instructions to their passengers. All this fun and they still please shareholders and win every major airline award.[2]

Myth #6: You Have to Have a Good Sense of Humor (Or Be Funny) to Create a Fun Work Environment

You may not be like Herb Kelleher. Many terrific bosses are not necessarily funny (or even very fun-loving). In many cases, they simply allow others' humor and playfulness to come out. They *support* rather than create fun at work. Let others initiate the kicks if it is not your strength.

> *My favorite boss was not necessarily a fun-loving person. She was pretty task-oriented and serious most of the time. One time she did dress up for Halloween and we were all completely shocked. That was a real stretch for her. Most of the time she just let us have our fun, without judging or squelching it.*
>
> —Supervisor, hospital

You might bring fun into your workplace by having brown bag lunches with unique and interesting speakers and topics. During a hobby-sharing lunch, one employee took everyone to a local park to demonstrate his remote-controlled airplanes. Another brought a local merchant to give a session on wine tasting. Another invited the local golf pro to give everyone a lesson.

Funny Makes Money

Fun breeds creativity. Add a little fun to the work environment and energy goes up. With that, productivity goes up. With that, innovation goes up. With that, new ideas are developed and money comes in. (Well, it's not *quite* that simple. But it happens.)

> *In 1995, managers at Irvine-based Fluor Corp. invited a group of gifted children from a local school to a management training meeting. The children sat with one group of executives, while a second group of Fluor managers worked independently. At day's end, the mixed group of executives and children had generated far more innovative ideas than the executives-only group.[3]*

BOTTOM LINE

Experience in every size company proves it: fun enhances creativity, and it certainly does not diminish productivity when everyone's work goals are clear. Let fun happen. Do not get in the way of your employees' creating kicks for themselves. That fun will energize, motivate and keep them on your team. And help fun to happen—get involved and create kicks with your employees. Support fun, encourage it, even reward it.

Chapter 12

LINK

Create Connections

*I found very little opportunity to meet anyone outside of my imme-
diate work unit. And my work unit seemed to be made up of a lot of
lone rangers.*

—A.J.

How much does your organization fit the "easy to leave" profile? It's easy
to leave a workplace:

✓ Where you feel no connection
✓ Where you have no group of colleagues who can offer support,
  information, or plain old gripe sessions
✓ If it is difficult to move your ideas through the pipeline
✓ If you do not have a set of relationships that enable you to get your
  work done
✓ If you don't look forward to seeing the people with whom you
  interact

Are You a Linker or Nonlinker?

A *nonlinker* thinks: If I link my employees to other functions or departments, someone there will steal them.

A *linker* thinks: If I don't link my employees to other functions or departments, their knowledge and skills are less likely to grow. My employees' productivity will be limited to the resources of their own department. Their work may become too function-focused for overall success.

Where can you start building links between your employees and the "communities" within your own organization? Just about anywhere. Link 'em to:

✓ The organization as a whole
✓ The department
✓ The team
✓ The professional community

Linking to the Organization

You don't need to work for the American Red Cross or Greenpeace to build a meaningful connection between the employee and the mission of the organization. When individuals understand and share the organization's purpose, their commitment grows.

Sometimes all this takes is discussion about the history of the company, its founders, its reason for being, the important needs it meets, or what customers say the company has done for them through its product line or service.

> *One medical device manufacturer brought in patients from a local hospital whose lives were saved or enhanced thanks to the company's product. All employees at all levels attended these meetings and were able to ask questions of these users. Employees swelled with pride and deepened their link to the organization. How might a meeting like this enhance the retention factor?*

Meetings with the president, CEO or other senior leaders are critical to linking employees with an organization's purpose. While mission statements capture the underlying principles of the organization and seldom change, the goals of the organization are incredibly dynamic. Keep employees abreast of these organization-wide changes to help them feel connected. If employees hear about changes (good or bad) in passing, they may feel out of the loop and start the dreaded rumor mill.

> *The Federal Reserve Bank of New York helps people connect within the organization with a social group called the Federal Reserve Club. It sponsors trips in which employees of all functions, titles, and levels may participate. This gives employees who wouldn't normally interact daily the opportunity to talk with each other informally. When an employee needs some information from another department, it's likely that he'll have a contact and won't be afraid to pick up the phone.*

One way to find organizational links is to list all the interdepartmental meetings you attend in a week. (Does the list give you a headache?) Decide in which of these meetings you might involve a member of your team. You will even free up some time on your own schedule in the process.

see OPPORTUNITIES

How do you create a bond among the employees in the department and increase the chances of deepening their loyalty? There are many ways.

TO DO . . .

✓ *Have open forum meetings on a regular basis.* If employees feel they are being heard, they will feel a stronger connection to you and the group. Don't be afraid of grievances either. Even if you can't do anything to fix the problem, people feel better just having the opportunity to talk it out.

✓ *Encourage group outings regularly*, and don't expect your group to do this on their own time. Consider allowing one paid afternoon per month—as long as it's a team activity.

✓ *Give employees time to talk.* Managers are often so worried about work not getting done that they discourage personal conversations among their staff. What they don't seem to understand is that these conversations help employees feel connected to each other.

✓ *Host informal breakfasts.* Your department needs to make informal connections occasionally. In a semisocial atmosphere you can introduce a new project, get creative juices flowing, and just kick off a new month.

Linking to the Team

Have you ever really felt like you were part of a team? Some of us may have to remember back to childhood playgrounds to recall the last time. If individuals supported each other on organizational teams the way they do on great sports teams, imagine the results.

> *Rhino Foods, a small company in Burlington, Vermont, creates teams for specific projects. Opportunity postings alert employees from all different parts of the business to project openings throughout the company. The result is a diverse team with a unique combined perspective rather than a one-dimensional group that always does things the same way.*[1]

Strong relationships at work are key to retaining your people. Most of us want and need colleagues to think with, work with and create with. Some surprising research reveals that coworker support is a key to retaining engineers. Yes, engineers. Those folks whom we often think of as task oriented and sometimes almost antisocial (how stereotypical!). The study found that engineers depend on the workplace as a primary source of social relationships.[2] The same is true for many of your key employees.

Alas

The competition offered me a 10 percent salary increase, and I took it. My boss was blown away by my resignation. He thought that I loved my job and had no idea that I could be enticed away. So what grabbed me?

Frankly, it was a combination of things. I felt no real connection to my workplace or the team. Maybe if we had spent a little more time together, or I had felt more a part of things there, I might have stayed. The company I'm joining operates primarily in teams. I'm hoping that will provide more of the interaction that I'm looking for. So the money was attractive, but the chance to be part of a team mattered even more.

—Engineer, aerospace firm

Had the manager known about this employee's need, he might have been able to create a better sense of team in the organization.

Linking to the Professional Community

Professional associations give people a chance to helicopter up from their own organization and learn what is happening elsewhere. How are other professionals handling similar problems and pressures? What unique approach worked in their culture?

The nonlinker's fear is that employees at a professional meeting might think the grass is greener. What if they get job offers? What if their association interests pull them further away from the job? All possible. But all this is still possible *even if* you don't support their involvement. Encourage your employees to join professional associations.

Why Teach Your Employees to Link?

As organizations abandon their hierarchical structures, managers will have to rely less on the authority inherent in their title and

more on their relationships with players in their informal networks.
Understanding relationships will be the key to managerial success.
—David Krackhardt and Jeffrey Hanson[3]

Better-linked employees can actually improve *your* links. Their expanding networks can provide you with new information and resources and can potentially increase the productivity of your entire team.

Here are some things you might do to help support and build professional connections for your team:

TO DO . . .

✓ Offer paid memberships in professional associations as a reward for work well done.

✓ Set aside time at staff meetings for your team to report on conferences or events they attend.

✓ Offer to bring several of your people with you to your meetings.

✓ Offer to speak at one of their association meetings.

✓ Ask all who have memberships in associations to contribute their association newsletters or journals to a reading table. Devote some time at a staff meeting to discussing and debating articles from one or more of these.

We know that you can't build these connections *for* your employees. But you can take steps to model and encourage connective possibilities for them.

How Can You Teach Your Employees to Link?

Perhaps A.J. left the organization because no link existed. You could prevent that by asking your employees whether any of the following sounds appealing.

TO DO . . .

Ask employees whether they would like to:

✓ Get straight feedback
✓ Learn a specific skill
✓ Hear about opportunities
✓ Get information
✓ Get help with an idea
✓ Get a specific job
✓ Gain visibility
✓ Find new contacts

Then ask yourself who else—inside or beyond your organization—could meet each employee's need. Link each employee to the person most able to fill his or her need by looking for these skills:

✓ *Nurturing.* Find someone who's able to listen and is there to support the individual as he or she makes choices. As their manager, it may be difficult for you to nurture your own employees. Encourage them to build personal relationships with others. Once the friendships are in place, the nurturing follows.

✓ *Sponsoring.* Find someone who can help them gain visibility and exposure, maybe even recommend them for a new job. While you can be a sponsor for your employee yourself, you may also want to direct the person to a colleague or superior who might offer something different.

✓ *Teaching.* Find someone who can help an employee learn a new skill. This may be a short-term teaching experience or a long-term, ongoing association. As a manager, you cannot be the only teacher for your entire staff. Match your employees with individuals who have different skill sets to ensure shared learning.

see INFORMATION

✓ *Informing.* Find someone who has information about what's going on inside or outside the organization and is able to share it. Remember, some of your colleagues are closer to the power sources than you are . . . and other people have different connections from yours.

✓ *Advising.* Find a person who is in a position to give good advice, someone who has seen it, been there, done that. The more you can point out these good advice givers the better.[4]

Tell Them the Secret of Reciprocity

Suggest that your employees always offer something in return. The Latin expression *quid pro quo* means "something for something," or in a more contemporary translation, "if you do something for me, I'll do something for you." If linking is only used to ask something of others, it will become one-sided and self-serving.

We often hear stories of "elegant currencies"—things you can offer that are easy for you that the other person needs but lacks resources to do. For example, you can teach somebody a new computer program. You can tell someone about a book you've read that could be invaluable to their work, or even summarize it for them. There are a myriad of ways that people can offer something in return.

TO DO . . .

Quid Pro Quo **Menu.** Services to offer your "links" in return:[5]

✓ Introduction to others (example: a potential client or supplier)

✓ Provide original ideas (example: a new way to process orders)

✓ Help others brainstorm (example: creative new ways to market a product)

✓ Volunteer help (example: at the other's charitable event)

✓ Increase other's networks (example: provide names of contacts the other needs)

- ✓ Reduce other's workloads (example: offer to help write part of a proposal)
- ✓ Offer feedback (example: suggest ways to improve the marketing brochure)
- ✓ Recommend to others (example: market product by word of mouth)
- ✓ Share expertise (example: computer skills)

BOTTOM LINE

Connections are a major reason people say they stay with organizations. If links are weak or nonexistent, leaving is easier. In the constantly changing work environment, it is up to you to strengthen whatever bonds you can between the people who work for you and others in the organization. Their links will strengthen yours—in a great *quid pro quo*—and they'll be more likely to stay.

Chapter 13

 **ENTOR**

Be One

I wish I'd had a mentor to coach me about some of the political land-mines that, quite frankly, I stepped on more than once!

—A.J.

FLASH! Check this item that appeared in *Business Week*:

Too caught up in meetings and business trips to give your star employee some career-related TLC? If so, you're making a mistake. Data from the 1999 Emerging Workforce Study show that 35 percent of employees who don't receive regular mentoring plan to look for another job within 12 months. But just 16 percent of those with good mentors expect to jump ship.[1]

This mentor stuff is not complex. What employees want in a mentor is often precisely what they want in a manager who cares. So here are some recommendations for mentoring behaviors that you can apply here and now. The more you act like a mentor to your direct reports, the more they will give second thoughts to leaving. Take Mari, for example:

I was keenly aware that my company didn't pay the highest wages for the job I do. At times it nagged at me. I would say to myself, "You know, you could get much more money for this job somewhere else."

One day, I decided to draw up a chart of the pluses and minuses of my job. I started to realize how many opportunities I had to learn. My boss was really good at knowing when I was ready to go to the next level, and she always offered the next step of learning, even before I would think of it. I was able to get exposure to other divisions and serve on multifunctional task teams. My manager took time to talk with me about success and about how to do things better. When I made my list, I realized how far I had come in a couple of years. I decided to stay because I didn't believe that all this would be easy to find in another company.

So What's a Mentor To Do?

Model   Be aware of your own role modeling, and point out others who are good role models for your people.

Encourage   Support your people in the risk taking that is essential to their growth.

Nurture   Get to know your people, their unique skills, and capabilities; work with them to do the most with their talents.

Teach   Tell it like it is. Help them avoid those organizational
Organizational   minefields that are never written about in any policy
Reality   manual.

Coping Models and Masterful Models

A wonderful maxim buried deep in management literature suggests that people are more likely to trust "copers" than "masters." People who cope aren't always successful and don't always get it right the first time. People who master never seem to step off the path and always have it together. If you believe that your people need to see you as having the answers, making no mistakes, then this first step of the mentoring process will be the most difficult.

One of us attended a parenting class recently. A world-class lecturer on effective parenting asked the group of 200 (many of whom were older parents) what they thought was the one (highly researched) way to definitely raise self-esteem in children. Hands went up. No one hit the jackpot. The speaker said that the ability of the parent to say "I made a mistake" had the greatest effect on the self-esteem of children. The speaker then asked the audience how many remember their parents ever uttering those words. Not many hands went up.

So our question is, how *real* can you afford to be? We think the answer is "pretty real." For example, let's say you were unable to hold to a predetermined agenda at an important meeting. Debriefing with an employee (Here's what I think happened: Did you see how I was sidetracked by Max's question?) is a wonderful way of mentoring.

Modeling as a mentoring behavior means watching for opportunities to show how you've coped, giving permission to others to do the same.

Just-In-Time Encouragement

Encouragement truly is all in the eye of the perceiver. For example, an employee says "He never encouraged me" while her manager says "I encouraged her all the time." How can you encourage effectively?

Clearly, attention and retention go hand in hand. It's easier for those who *have* been encouraged.

Some managers encourage naturally, through casual conversations. Here's the easiest approach to offering encouragement, just in time. There are three steps:

1. *Recognize:* Notice something.
2. *Verbalize:* Say something.
3. *Mobilize:* Do something.[2]

see CAREERS

Any of the three steps will encourage, but all three combined are much more powerful. Following are examples based on this situation: Liliana gives a beautifully designed flyer to her manager and says, "I've been doing some fiddling with that new graphics program and laser printer."

Recognize. Manager: "Hmm, looks great. I didn't know you like this kind of stuff." (Good.)

Recognize and Verbalize. Manager: "This is really good. Is this something you'd like to do more of?" (Better.)

Recognize, Verbalize and Mobilize. Manager: "If you like this kind of work, why not let Marc in Graphics know, and while you're there, find out when he's offering his next graphics course." (Best.)

Impromptu mentoring of this type is even more important if your sit-down time is really constrained. For many employees, these simple interactions will send a strong message that they matter.

Nurturing on the Run

Countless employees who have left their corporations say that their managers never stopped long enough to understand them or support them in their development.

Alas

From an interview with a senior level manager in a high-tech company:

Interviewer: *Did you ever have a mentor?*
Manager: *You bet. He was my manager. He really cared about me. He'd stop in all the time, ask me some great questions, get me to think about what I was doing and why. He gave me some great strokes, and kept my juices flowing.*
Interviewer: *Do you do that for anyone?*
Manager: *No—I would like to, but we don't really have the time these days.*

Mentoring takes time, but not a lot. Mainly it takes willingness to show another person that you genuinely care.

Nurture Ideas. When employees come to you with suggestions or ideas about how they might approach something differently, do you move immediately to no? Do you kill an idea before it is even off the tongue? (Tell the truth!) We hear that employees feel put down and turned down far more than their managers are aware. And that makes leaving easier. Instead, try listening to the entire idea, try playing with it as a "what if." Ask for more information. Sleep on it, mull it over. Think, "Isn't that interesting" *before* you think, "It will never work."

Nurture Relationships. Get to know your employees and give them every opportunity to get to know you.

> *A senior marketing VP at a top-ten Fortune company commented that she wished managers in her organization would recognize how important a relationship with them was to their people. "And I don't mean anything deep," she said. "It's the little things, like a cup of coffee together once in a while." Employees want to feel they count and are noticed. When they feel invisible, it's easy for them to leave.*

Managers who seize every opportunity to nurture the talented people on their team are the managers who will keep those people.

Teach Organizational Reality

Everyone knows at least one sad story of a technically brilliant employee with everything to offer who derailed because of political blunders, lack of interpersonal skills, or ignorance of the unwritten rules. Countless corporate advice books suggest that academic brilliance alone does not make success. Daniel Goleman talks about EQ (emotional quotient—your ability to empathize, to relate to your peers). Paul Stoltz refers to AQ (adversity quotient—your ability to deal with bad luck or plans gone wrong). Others point to arrogance, insensitivity to others or managing upward instead of down as career stoppers. Your ability and willingness to *tell it like it is* can save a career, perhaps for the benefit of your own organization.

Alas

She was technically brilliant. She graduated in the top two percent of her class in one of the top schools in the country. She was pursued by all of our competitors. We won. We offered opportunities for her to continue on her fast track, to work with other brilliant colleagues, to sit on a variety of committees that made decisions on our future direction. We had great plans for her.

She was so quick, though, that she started to rub people the wrong way. She continually ignored our chain of command. She stepped on toes. No one gave her any alternative ways to deal with the folks whose respect she needed.

Slowly, her influence eroded. Although she continued to be way out there in terms of what she knew, she just couldn't manage to communicate with her team or her peers. People avoided her. She became more and more isolated. And she became more and more unhappy with our organization. Before we knew enough to try to talk it out, give her some help, we lost her."

—Manager, high-tech company

How do you talk about unwritten rules? What if you coach someone, talk about the buttons they press, and you are wrong? Your view is just your view. Could you mess it up even more? We don't think so.

We have never heard of a manager who mentored too much and thereby lost an employee. We've never heard of a manager who coached too often and thereby lost someone's trust. We've never heard of a manager who talked too frequently about how he or she saw the organizational world and failed to retain talent for that reason.

see TRUTH

Employees need to know your point of view. They want to know your take on how people get and give resources, what kinds of influence strategies work and don't work, what certain senior leaders want and don't want in their reports, their presentations, their meetings. And they want to know this *before* they walk into a minefield, or, at the very least, they want to be able to look at something that didn't work and understand why!

A general manager in a worldwide chemical company participated in a group mentoring program. His responsibility was to meet with a group of high-potentials once a month for two hours and talk with them about whatever issues seemed important. He had one favorite question to put to each group, and he loved the dialogue that followed. He said, "I have a theory I call PIE. It's a success theory. Which part of the PIE do you think is most important? Performance? Image? Or Exposure?" He delighted in hearing the young brilliant chemical engineers all yell, "It's performance!"

"No," he would say defiantly, "it is definitely not performance. We take that for granted. The greatest mark of success is Image and Exposure." The engineers hated that. They fought him every step of the way. They could not believe that this fluffy stuff could be so important, and it made them angry. But he stuck with it. He listened to their comments, acknowledged their rage. He explained that he felt that way too when he began in the company.

Eventually each group got it. And they appreciated him for raising the issue and teaching them that not-so-pleasant lesson. Whether all of them heeded his words we don't know. Those that did were probably more successful. But all appreciated the discussion and his candor. They never forgot it.

So if you are nodding your head, consider using one of your own staff meetings to open a dialogue on organizational reality.

TO DO . . .

Invite your team to talk about any of the following questions.

- ✓ What have I learned about what counts in this organization?
- ✓ How have my failures and successes grown me?
- ✓ What most surprised me about the culture?
- ✓ What was the most difficult culture shift for me to make?
- ✓ What are the ways to really get in hot water here?
- ✓ How do people derail themselves?
- ✓ What do I know now that I wish I had known then?

There is a hunger for frank conversation in organizations today. Because of the intense competition, few employees feel that they can really express themselves or ask the questions that are really on their minds. Most people claim they do not like playing politics. But because it's a reality of corporate life, a mentor watches out for the organizational well-being of a protégé. A mentor educates, and through this education protects a protégé from stumbling. A manager who is intent on keeping talent can adapt some of these principles.

One More Thing

We saved this for last. Know one of the best ways of mentoring? Let your people mentor you. Let them tell you what they know. Ask them to tell you how they see the world. Let them coach you about how you might be more effective in *their* development. Observe. Stay open. You'll be amazed at how much you'll learn. And in the process of learning, you can't help but model, encourage, nurture and teach organizational reality.

BOTTOM LINE

Your employees want you to teach them the ropes—and they know their careers will suffer if you don't. The manager who is able to integrate mentoring behaviors into everyday work finds a strong payback in employee loyalty and retention.

Chapter 14

NUMBERS

Run Them

My friend's boss told her that she could be easily replaced with some-one he pays a lot less. He said it half-jokingly, but she knew that there was a serious side to his statement. She left because she wants to work for someone who values the work she does.

—A.J.

Imagine that you arrive at work one morning to the evidence of a burglary. A brand new desktop computer has disappeared from an employee's desk. You call the building security office and the police. Then you launch your own investigation. You are determined to find out how this happened and who is responsible. You will not rest until the case is solved. And you immediately increase security measures—no more property will be lost!

Now think about the last time one of your most talented employees was stolen by the competition or just walked out your door. What kind of investigation did you launch? What measures were implemented to prevent it from happening again? Maybe the loss of a $40,000–200,000 asset set off no alarm bells because no one ever really assessed the cost of losing talent. It doesn't take long to run the numbers. And you may be surprised.

Numbers and financial statements are the universal language of business. These are usually about cold, hard cash. Front-line workers and senior managers alike understand them. A careful assessment of the numbers might just convince you to focus more heavily on retaining your talent!

What's the Price Tag?

You may think they are easily replaced—those dedicated, talented people who have been critical to your success. And yes, you might even find replacements at lower salaries. We hear this argument often, especially during periods of high unemployment when many good people are looking for work. Often, though, the managers who say this have simply not calculated the real costs of turnover. Research suggests that replacing a key person on your staff will cost you between 70 and 200 percent of the person's compensation.

Alas

John was one of our most talented engineers and was responsible for inventing some of our key technology. He asked his boss for a 15 percent raise (about $15,000) and his boss immediately said, "Forget it!" John did and left the organization to join a competitor who was thrilled to pay him 30 percent more than he had been making. Some said, "Oh well, we'll replace him within weeks."

Here's what actually happened:

✔ *We hired a headhunter for $40,000 to try to steal someone like John from a competitor.*

✔ *After a three-month search, we found five good candidates and flew them all in for interviews at a total cost of $5,000.*

(continued)

✓ We selected the new guy (after much wining/dining and selling) and agreed to a sign-on bonus of $10,000 and a moving allowance of $25,000. His salary was negotiated at 25 percent above John's ($20,000 difference in the first year.)

So the bottom line in salary and expenses looked like about $100,000 to get the new guy in the door. But wait, that's not all.

✓ Our competitor won John (including his brilliant brain and technical knowledge) and went on to win a multibillion dollar contract that would have been ours.

✓ John's buddies all started looking around and the company executives got wind of it. Senior leadership decided to give them a 15 percent raise for two years in a row. (Cost = $200,000)

✓ We lost two or three other key people to competitors. Their technical expertise went with them. Our cutting-edge technology leaked out the doors and we made our competition stronger almost overnight.

So it wasn't a $100,000 cost after all. It was literally billions. And this does not take into account the harder-to-measure costs of lowered morale, discontent and lowered productivity following John's departure. In hindsight it is clear we should have worked a little harder to keep John. We should have paid him what he was worth in the market, but also made certain that he was challenged and happy with his day-to-day work. Losing him was a very costly mistake.

—Manager, high-tech company

This story may seem unusual. Certainly not every employee is worth billions to your bottom line. However, the story is true and illustrates the principle we are talking about. No one other than the manager in this story ran the numbers to figure out what losing John actually cost.

Managers seldom do, because then they would have to look for the real causes of turnover or find somewhere to place blame. They might even begin to create retention strategies. Most leaders just don't want to do all that.

You will never really know what it costs to lose a talented employee if the cost is never calculated!

With the real cost of losing talent in mind, here is what we recommend. Use the following grid to assess the cost of replacing one of your excellent employees who left for another job. We have left blanks for you to add items that are relevant in your organization.

Item	Cost
Newspaper ads	_____
Search firm	_____
Interview costs: airlines, hotels, meals, etc.	_____
Manager and team members' time spent interviewing	_____
Work put on hold until replacement is on board	_____
Overload on team, including overtime to get the work done during selection and training of replacement	_____
Orientation and training time for replacement	_____
Lost customers	_____
Lost contracts or business	_____
Lowered morale and productivity, time spent talking about it around the water cooler	_____
Sign-on bonus and other perks	_____
Moving allowance	_____
Loss of other employees	_____
_____	_____

_____ _____

_____ _____

_____ _____

In addition to running the numbers using the grid, you might want to ponder these questions:

✓ How much money would your organization save if it reduced turnover by 1 percent?
✓ How would your organization use those dollars if they did not have to be spent on recruiting, hiring and training new employees? (Consider employee development, enrichment programs, bonuses, incentives, or research and development.)

BOTTOM LINE

Retaining your best employees can be viewed as a strictly rational business strategy. In business terms, you need to calculate the costs of losing and replacing key talent. For those who believe in the "easy come, easy go" philosophy of hiring and turnover, assessing these costs objectively can sharpen your commitment to keeping your most valuable employees.

Chapter 15

OPPORTUNITIES

Mine Them

I didn't see any great looking choices there. The truth is, I didn't look very hard for other options in the company and neither did my manager.

—A.J.

Talented people have many choices about where they work. To keep them, learn how to "opportunity mine" with them. This *does not* mean that you are in charge of their career paths. It is not up to you to find their next exciting job. But if you really want to retain them, you must help them find opportunities *right here at home.*

Alas

Lynne was a rising star, destined to do great things for the team—and her great work always made her supervisor look great. When she gave notice and her manager asked why, she answered, "I've been very happy here. You're a terrific boss and the people are great. It's just that I'm ready

(continued)

for something new, and this opportunity popped up in another company. I wasn't really looking for it; it just happened. I've decided to go for it."

The manager felt absolutely sick about losing her. What on earth would the team do? He offered more money, but the lure of this new, exciting opportunity had her already mentally and emotionally out the door. And when the manager probed a bit, he realized that the very opportunity she was leaving for was available within the department. Responsibility rests on both sides. She didn't look and her manager didn't direct her.

Avoid that scenario and keep your talent through a three-step process that we call opportunity mining. Before you consider the three steps, consider your own views on opportunities at work.

Are You Opportunity High or Opportunity Shy?

To discover opportunities, one must look at the world in a new way, through a new lens. It is impossible to make people smarter, but you can help them see with new eyes.
—Gary Hamel, Harvard Business Review, August 1996

What do we mean by being opportunity minded or by opportunity mining? Opportunity mindedness describes a state of mind and a set of beliefs, attitudes and behaviors. It is opportunism in the most positive sense of the word.

Opportunity mining means looking for, finding and then retrieving opportunities. Its three key behaviors are seeking, seeing and seizing. (The opposite of an opportunity miner is an opportunity whiner—you know, the one who is constantly complaining about his lot in life and at work.)

As a manager, you can partner with your employees to opportunity mine. It may be helpful for you to begin by getting a feel for your own level of opportunity mindedness. Complete the Opportunity Audit below to find out if you are *opportunity high* or *opportunity shy*.

OPPORTUNITY AUDIT[1]

Using the following scale, jot down the number that best indicates the extent to which each statement is true for you: 1 = Rarely, 2 = Sometimes, 3 = Usually, 4 = Always.

I am at ease when considering other people's viewpoints. _____

I seek and implement new technologies for improving
efficiency and output. _____

I know the trends in the marketplace; I could tell you what
competitors are doing and why. _____

I take an active role in professional group(s). _____

I tap into other people to help launch and support my
career growth. _____

I am flexible about adjusting plans when the first or second
attempts at something fail. _____

I am quite comfortable interpreting the "gray" areas of policy
and practices. _____

I let career interests be known through formal (e.g., job
posting) and informal (e.g., conversation) channels. _____

I know how to connect people and information, and others
seek my help in gaining access or information. _____

How did you do? If you are opportunity high (scoring over 27), you are probably already seeking, seeing and seizing opportunities for yourself and maybe even with and for your employees. If you scored on the low end (anything less than 18), you might benefit from the suggestions that follow. Only the opportunity-minded manager can truly help employees find possibilities for themselves.

> *There is no security on this earth; there is only opportunity.*
> —Douglas MacArthur[2]

Seeking Opportunities

> **Seek:** *To make a search for; to try to reach or obtain; to attempt.*
> —Webster's Dictionary

Too many employees and too many managers walk around their organization not searching for opportunities. Or they seem to notice only the negative news or the black cloud on every bright horizon. Your willingness to seek will model this positive action for your employees. *It's important for you as well.*

TO DO . . .

✓ In a meeting with your employees, read a front-page newspaper article with a negative title (shouldn't be hard to find one of those!). Now ask them to scan the article and search for any positive words, lines or themes in the midst of the negative news. Sometimes it is difficult, but it's seldom impossible to find a speck of good news hidden in the bad. It may be like finding the proverbial needle in the haystack. Whether or not you and your team members found the good news in the article, you just exercised *seeking*.

Opportunity-minded managers constantly scan the horizon for possibilities, both for themselves *and* for their people. They ask employees about the types of opportunities they might be looking for and may even help them look. (Yes, even if it means some good folks leave the team.)

> *Trident Data Systems is an opportunity-rich organization where managers are opportunity seekers. They have developed a culture where employees feel comfortable speaking up when they are getting bored or need/want a new challenge, a promotion or a different type of work. Employee development meetings are held regularly, where managers come to the table to discuss their employees' interests and desires. They surface new possibilities and link employee goals with opportunities that already exist or are on the horizon. After several years the results have been measurably positive. Not only do they retain their talented people, but their recruiting efforts have been greatly enhanced, as interviewees see Trident as an opportunity-rich organization.*

While Trident launched this process in a formal, systemwide approach, it doesn't have to be done that way. You can do it yourself.

Hold development meetings with your employees where the only topic is their career and what opportunities they might be seeking. "What if there are no opportunities here?" you ask. "What if I just open a can of worms by asking my employees what they are seeking? And what if I simply cannot help them, or by opening the conversation I encourage them to leave?" To answer these tough questions, put yourself in their shoes. How do you feel about a boss who wants to help you seek opportunities for yourself? What happens to your level of respect and commitment while you work for him or her? What happens to your sense of loyalty to this boss and even to the team or company? It all goes *up!*

Check with managers in other departments to find out where new possibilities lie. Brainstorm with your employees to surface opportunities to enrich the jobs they currently hold. Be proactive about it. And remember: You won't see it 'til you seek it.

Seeing Opportunities

See: *To perceive or have the power of sight; to comprehend, to have a mental picture of.*

—Webster's Dictionary

TO DO ...

What does this title mean?

Opportunityisnowhere

✓   Opportunity is now here.
✓   Opportunity is nowhere.
✓   Opportunity I snow here. (You're in trouble if you picked this one!)

Most of us immediately lock on to one perspective and remain fairly confident in our findings. You may have chosen the first answer or the second and did not even consider the possibility that there is another point of view. Try this with your people. It is a great opener to a discussion of opportunities.

Just as you may have seen a different phrase from your employee or colleague in the exercise, you may see plenty of opportunities in the organization while your talented employee sees none.

If you are an opportunity-minded manager, you will help your employees *seek* opportunities but will also help them to *see* those opportunities when they are right in front of their faces. You can shed the right light, point out the features and distinctions, turn the opportunity around or upside down to make it more visible. Best yet, you will teach your employees how to do those things for themselves.

In partnership with your employees, ask: Where and how carefully are we looking?

Raychem has an insiders' network of over 360 people across the organization who are willing to take the time to talk with any employee who wants to learn about the nature of their work and the requirements of their jobs. This network has a computerized database (called Internal Information Interview Network) with the names and backgrounds of all the employees who participate. [3]

What a great way to share information about opportunities. And what a great way to see if a pasture that looks greener really *is* greener. If you don't have such a database, you can still send folks who are wondering (and wandering) out to interview or e-mail people you know in other areas. Apple lets employees see by offering them the opportunity to fill in for those on a sabbatical. The option is available to all employees. Could you do this?

TO DO . . .

✓ Look around to see what is changing in your department, division or organization. What new projects are on the horizon? What department is expanding, which one shrinking? Who might be retiring soon or leaving for a new opportunity, and therefore opening up a promotional or learning possibility for one of your stars? Talk about these potential opportunities with your employees. Look carefully, dig deeply for possible opportunities.

Seizing Opportunities

Seize: To take possession or hold of quickly and forcibly; to take eagerly.

—Webster's Dictionary

Many people are quite good at both seeking and seeing opportunities even when they are camouflaged. But many of us are not so good at the most critical behavior of the opportunity-minded person: *seizing*. We may look for and see an opportunity, but something prevents us from acting, from reaching out and grabbing it. For example, you may know someone who has a list of stocks or property they almost bought, a sport they almost learned or a trip almost taken.

If you scored opportunity-high on the Opportunity Audit, you probably seek, see and seize quite well. If you want to retain your top talent, help them learn to seize opportunities that come their way. What are the barriers to seizing opportunities? It may be helpful to figure out why your employees fail to act and what you might do to help them.

TO DO . . .

✓ If your employees did not create a plan of action, you could help them do so. These plans should have concrete tactical action steps with time lines, potential obstacles and support needed (what kind and by whom).

✓ If your employees did not adhere to their plans (too busy, resources delayed, etc.), you could help them adhere to their plans. Suggest regular check-point meetings to discuss progress and brainstorm solutions to obstacles along the way.

✓ If your employees second-guessed themselves (analysis paralysis), you could help them avoid this. With their agreement, point out second-guessing behaviors that are more apt to be delay tactics than true assessment. Again, with permission, push for action when enough analysis has taken place.

✓ If your employees decided a particular opportunity was just not for them, you could help them decide if it truly is not the right choice. After careful assessment, some opportunities are best passed by.

✓ If your employees let others talk them out of it, you could help them be strong in the face of naysayers and risk-averse "friends" and colleagues. Those people may be opportunity-shy (and sometimes even opportunity whiners).

✓ If your employees were just plain afraid to act, you could help them face the fear and just do it! Sometimes we just need an ally to provide support and a measure of courage when we get the jitters. Talk about the *what-ifs* with them—what if you try it and it doesn't work out? Usually the risks are not really life-threatening, even though they may feel like it.

He who refuses to embrace a unique opportunity loses the prize as surely as if he tried and failed.

—William James[4]

BOTTOM LINE

Our research shows that, more than any other single factor, people stay in an organization because of opportunities to stretch, grow and learn.

If you hope to keep your talent on your team, you must become opportunity minded, an opportunist in the positive sense of the word, on behalf of your people. If they come to you wanting something new or something more, partner with them to find opportunities. Be glad that you have ambitious opportunity miners on your team. Be forewarned, too. If you can't help them to seek, see and seize opportunities at home, you will certainly lose them to organizations that can.

Chapter 16

 **P**ASSION

Encourage It

The work was okay, but my heart wasn't in it.

—A.J.

Show your employees that you care about them by helping them find work they love to do. It may not always be easy, and you may even risk losing some of them. But if you don't partner with your talented employees to find work they are passionate about, you will no doubt lose them anyway.

People Are Passionate

What are your employees passionate about? What gets each of them up in the morning with a feeling of anticipation and eagerness about the day? When we asked dozens of people about their work passions, here is some of what we heard:

- ✓ "I love creating something new. Something no one has ever seen or even imagined before."
- ✓ "I get a kick out of working on such an elite team. There is so much brilliance here."

✓ "I love drawing, welding, building something."

✓ "I love numbers. I'd rather work with them than with people."

✓ "I really get excited when I discover a new rule in math."

✓ "I love to help someone get better at something and get happier in the process."

✓ "I love managing others. What a kick it is to motivate and guide a team to do great things."

✓ "My passion is turnaround—taking something that is broken and fixing it."

The responses are certainly diverse. Yet a common theme surfaces: When people are doing what they love, they are at their best. If you help connect your employees' passions to their jobs, you and they will reap the rewards.

"Just Be Glad You Have a Job"

During decades of corporate downsizing, we heard many managers use this phrase with the dissatisfied employees who remained in the organization. For many employees, the thrill was gone. Broken relationships and broken promises caused apathy and a sense of sadness for thousands. As a result, many employees spent years doing work that felt boring or meaningless. Some researchers have estimated that those people leave half of their heart and brain in bed and a quarter of both in the car (or train or bus) when they arrive at work. As a result, they show up in your workplace with about 25 percent. How are you supposed to win with that?

> In some ways I quit and stayed. I am so apathetic about the work that I am doing, that I put in the bare minimum effort. They could get so much more from me if I were doing work that I love.
> —Front-line worker, manufacturing

Somehow you need to corral the greatest possible percentage of each employee's heart and head. In addition to this challenge, many of you struggle to recruit and retain top talent in a time of high employment and rampant talent theft. Employees have choices, and you can bet the most talented (and sought after) will seek work that they love.

Uncover and Discover

So what can you do to help people find work that gives them a thrill? First, ask. Ask several ways because people respond differently to different words. Try, "What work do you really love to do?" or "What are you passionate about?" or "What gives you the greatest thrill or kicks at work?" As they answer, dig a little deeper. Then think creatively about how their passions might be used in the workplace.

see ASK

When one manager had the passion conversation with his employee, here is how it went:

Manager: What do you love to do? What are you passionate about?

Tara: I've recently learned to use some desktop publishing software and I've created some brochures for my church. I'm having a ball with it.

Manager: I wonder if there is a way we could use your talent and interest here at work.

Tara: I've been thinking about it and wondered if I could take on the layout of the new company newsletter we've been talking about.

Manager: How would that work out with your current heavy workload?

Tara: I will definitely get my work done. You know that about me. This project will be above and beyond my current workload.

Manager: Let's give it a try. Keep me posted as you work on the first issue. Let me know what's working and what's not.

Tara was feeling pretty bored with her job. She'd been doing the same work for years and the thrill was gone. She had even been thinking of leaving. She poured herself into the new project, teamed with

see ENRICH

colleagues, and turned out a dynamite first newsletter. Her teammates and boss praised her and were truly astounded at her accomplishment.

Since that event, Tara has expanded her job to include multiple graphic arts projects. Her boss worked with her to restructure the job and hand off some of her former duties to other people. Tara's energy and productivity have soared, and she wakes up *eager* to go to work. Her job has been enriched by the new activities. The key to her renewed enthusiasm is that her boss collaborated with her to uncover and then capitalize on her passion.

What if passion lies outside of work? Some people are more passionate about skiing or about their children than about their work. What do you do then? Think about how the workplace might accommodate or flex to allow them to do more of what they love. Telecommuting, flex hours and on-site day-care centers are all strategies that support peoples' passions.

> *I can't imagine leaving this job. The day-to-day work is good and the team is great. But one of the best aspects of my job is that some of us go skiing most Fridays. We work hard all week to get the work done. We sometimes work evenings and even on the weekend when necessary. Then we take off. Skiing is my passion and this job allows me to enjoy it every week. How many of those jobs are there?*
>
> —Accountant, software company

This highly productive employee will continue to produce for his boss and team. That's the payback for his manager's flexibility.

TO DO . . .

✓ Ask your employees what they love to do. What are they passionate about?

✓ Dig deeper. Really understand what they are saying to you.

✓ Get creative. Collaborate with them to find ways to either:
  - Incorporate their passion in the work they do.
  - Flex the work somehow to allow time for their passion outside of work.

Meaningful Mission

Many people become passionate about a meaningful mission. It's not really the work that provides the thrill in many cases, but the result! Look at people washing cars to raise money for a great cause or those pounding nails to provide shelter for the homeless and you'll see what we mean. Managers who can paint a meaningful mission, a reason to do this work, seem to inspire great commitment to day-to-day tasks.

> *I've been the janitor and maintenance expert here for 30 years. I love my work. I help make this building beautiful and safe for the people who work here and the people who live here. We take care of old people who need nursing care and help with their daily living. They deserve the best, after all they have done and given in their lives. The director here gave me an award for my service and told everyone how critical I am to serving our residents. That award hangs on my wall at home.*
>
> —Maintenance expert, nursing home

This man is crystal clear about the value of his work. He is inspired by the mission of the organization and the reason for his being there.

Southwest Airlines provides another clear example of how the mission can inspire people to work with passion. One of its slogans is, "It's not a job, it's a crusade." The people of Southwest are crusaders who truly believe they are in the business of freedom. They make it possible for people to fly who could never afford to fly in the past.[1]

So what is your organization or team mission? How clearly is it stated and felt in your organization? Does it inspire a passionate approach to work?

TO DO . . .

✓ Articulate the mission of your organization or team. Why do you exist? What would be lost to the world if you went away tomorrow?
✓ Share that mission with your employees.
✓ Clearly link every employee's work to the mission. How does his/her work contribute to it? How important is she/he to you and to the mission of your team and organization?

Passion Busters

Once you and your employees have worked to discover their passions and to link their work to the organization's mission, it's time to remove the barriers. What gets in the way?

Alas

He loved training and teaching others and told me he wanted to do more of that. Every chance he had, he would volunteer to teach a class, any class, even if it wasn't technical training. He learned to facilitate a team-building process that proved to be very successful in his business unit. But I just couldn't free him up to do more of what he loved. He was one of our best engineers and we couldn't afford to have him pulled off his key projects to do this other work. How silly, in hindsight, that I was so protective of him and his time—now I have neither! He left us six months ago for a job that lets him utilize his talent and passion.

—Director, public utility

Organizational Constraints

Which organizational constraints interfere with giving your employees different work or more of the kind of work they love? The list is often lengthy and is sometimes called "reality." You might be thinking that this passion stuff sounds good on paper, but the reality is we don't have enough:

see QUESTION

✓ Time
✓ Money
✓ Staff
✓ Management support
✓ _____ (fill in the blank).

These constraints may be real. But remember, if you don't help your talented employees find work they love in your organization, you will lose them. Do you have enough time, money and staff to deal with their loss and replacement?

Self-Interest

When you help your best employees uncover and pursue their passions, it may mean they will need to leave you to pursue those dreams. Out of self-interest (sometimes team interest) you might tend to avoid the passion discussion for fear of losing them. Ironically, your odds of keeping those people are better when you collaborate with them to find exciting, meaningful work right where they are.

My passion was the volunteer work I was doing in my community. My evenings and weekends were spent with a group that was working with the inner-city kids in Los Angeles. We were involved in mentoring them and providing safe playgrounds and educational opportunities. At work I honestly just showed up, did the minimum and then shot out of there at 5:00 P.M. sharp. I sat down with my boss one day and described the volunteer work that I was doing and how much it meant to me. He had a brilliant idea. He said that his boss had told him that the organization was committing to some new community outreach programs and that they were thinking of creating a new role in the organization. The next thing I knew, I became the director of community projects for our corporation. My work and my passion are now one and the same. As long as I can do this, I will never leave this organization!

—Director, entertainment company

The boss lost this employee from the team (it was inevitable)—but *saved* him for the organization.

TO DO ...

✓ Assess the organizational constraints that serve as passion busters. Are they real? How can you overcome them?

✓ Be honest about your self-interests. Get clear about the upsides/downsides of helping employees find work they love.

✓ Support and encourage your employees as they pursue their passion.

BOTTOM LINE

People who do what they love usually do it very, very well. If passion is missing at work, your best people may not bring their best to work. So collaborate with them to uncover and discover what they love to do. Link them and their work to your mission and help them remove the barriers to doing what they love. The payoffs for you are enthusiastic, productive employees who will stay and play on your team.

Chapter 17

QUESTION

Reconsider the Rules

I remember twice in the last year, coming up with some slightly unorthodox ways of approaching a problem. Each time I was told simply, "It would be against our rules to do it that way." I quit offering my ideas.

—A.J.

If innovation is so important to most organizations, why is it so hard to support? Why is it so easy to move to no, before saying yes? Why is it always easier to look first at the past to see if there is a precedent for what an employee wants to do?

It may be human nature, habit or fear that keeps most managers in the box, holding rigidly to the rules. Yet innovation happens when they venture *out* of the box and encourage their employees to do the same.

When your employees come to you with new ideas, concepts or rule breakers, they want to hear, "You've got a point," or "Let's give it a try," or "Maybe that will work." The chance to contribute creatively brings many people great satisfaction. They want to be recognized for their good ideas and innovative solutions and they want *you* to support their questioning. You will increase the odds of keeping talented employees by allowing them to question the rules about their jobs, the workplace and even the business.

A Rule's a Rule

The world would be even more chaotic if there were no rules. We count on rules to provide safety and sanity in our communities and workplaces. Yet most of us would agree that progress demands questioning the rules.

What if these people hadn't questioned the rules?

✓ *Wright Brothers:* Why can't people fly?
✓ *Steve Jobs:* Why can't everyone have their own computer?
✓ *Thomas Edison:* Why can't we create lights that turn on with a switch?
✓ *Fred Smith:* Why can't we move packages across the globe overnight?
✓ *Jonas Salk:* Why can't we prevent debilitating disease?

What if others hadn't asked:

✓ Why can't we go to the moon?
✓ Why can't we reclaim Lake Erie to its former glory?
✓ Why can't we use lasers to perform surgery?
✓ Why can't we share data instantly over long distances?
✓ Why can't we build a computer after it's ordered?
✓ Why can't we create radar-invisible aircraft and ships?

You get the idea. The rule questioners and ultimately the rule breakers are our innovators. They improve our lives and they are the backbone of successful organizations.

Alas

Darren was a new employee, hired to bring us fresh new ideas and an outside perspective. He began to annoy us during his first month on the new job. He kept asking us questions like, "Have you thought about doing it this way?" and "Why does this process take eight steps, when it could be four?" We held firmly to the way it had been done—why fix it if it ain't broken? Darren hung in there for six months and then shocked us all by leaving. He said the environment stifled his creativity and that new ideas were not appreciated here. The sad thing is he's right.

—Manager, medical technology firm

You might be thinking that Darren's timing was off. He could have waited for a few months before suggesting all those changes. Yet Darren would have thrived in a workplace that truly encourages innovation and creativity. His manager and teammates would have welcomed his early questions and suggestions for change. After all, isn't that why they hired him?

So how open are you to the questions your employees bring you?

TO DO . . .

Complete the following sentence to determine whether you are more like Manager A or Manager B.

When employees ask me to question the rules, I most often:

Manager A

❒ Give them a quick yes or no answer.

Manager B

❒ Tell them I would like to explore it further with them.

❐ Give them the reasons why we do it this way.

❐ Tell them I don't have time to deal with it.

❐ Suggest they ask someone else.

❐ Avoid justifying how we currently do it.

❐ Suggest a time frame for dealing with their question.

❐ Collaborate with them to find other resources if necessary.

If you are more like Manager A, you may be an action-oriented, highly productive individual. While you may have many excellent traits, you could be described as being a *question-unfriendly manager*. It won't take long for your employees to recognize that and do some or all of the following:

✓ Stop bringing you questions
✓ Shut down their creative, innovative brains
✓ Become less enthusiastic about work (and possibly less productive too)
✓ Leave you for a more inviting workplace where their questions are encouraged

If you are more like Manager B, you tend to respond eagerly and openly to your employees' questions. You are a *question-friendly manager*. You are used to thinking, "What if that worked?" or "Why not see if we could change that policy?" or "How could this idea make us more productive?" You spend time brainstorming with your employees and you collaborate with them to find answers to their questions.

Fifteen years ago (before flextime was popular), Barry went to his manager and asked if he could work a four-day week. He wanted to support his wife's growing business on the fifth day. That request was unusual and definitely represented a rule breaker, but his boss considered it carefully and worked to gain approval. Barry was a highly valued scientist and his boss did not want to lose him. It worked. Barry is still producing and innovating for that organization because his boss reconsidered the rules.

How would Barry's story play out in your workplace? What would have happened fifteen years ago? Think about the people who first asked similar questions about:

✓ Job sharing
✓ Flextime
✓ Telecommuting
✓ Casual dress
✓ Self-managed teams
✓ Childcare centers
✓ Employee ownership plans
✓ Maternity leaves

These are just a few of the workplace innovations that many employees now take for granted. If they are against the rules in your workplace, you might question those managers that could change this for you or your employees. Someone had the courage to ask questions about work and someone's manager listened and acted. Are you that kind of manager?

see UNDERSTAND

Are You Boxed In?

You have no doubt been asked (probably more than once) to think outside the box. How ironic that most managers feel like the box has been handed to them (often by their bosses) and that they are supposed to think and act inside of it! An old training exercise (source unknown) suggests that the box typically feels fairly rigid, as if it were made up of concrete walls—the rules. But a shift in thinking could have your box composed of different materials, each with unique properties. Here is an example:

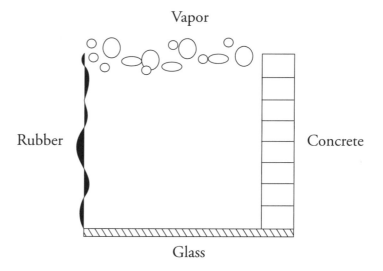

This box has walls made of four materials.

✓ **Concrete.** This wall represents rules that are truly rigid. It cannot be broken, pushed, bent or shattered. Example: *"You must have a medical degree to practice medicine in this hospital."*

✓ **Glass.** This wall is strong and sturdy, but if you hit it just the right way with just the right instrument at the right time, it will break. It represents the rules that may seem unbreakable but actually can be broken. Example: *"Women will never be Supreme Court Justices."*

✓ **Rubber.** This wall is thick and strong, but has some give to it if you are willing to push hard. It represents rules that might be bendable. Example: *"We all put in a forty-hour week, from eight to five, five days a week."*

✓ **Vapor.** This wall is made up of our beliefs, assumptions and perceptions about the rules. Example: *"People will never fly."*

If you examine the rules you operate by, you will find that few of them are truly concrete. They just feel that way. The most formidable aspect of the box is often the vapor wall. Your beliefs and assumptions—

or the company's—will often prevent you from questioning the rules. They may close you to your employees' questions as well.

SportsMind is an organization that specializes in experiential learning and high-performance team building for managers. One exercise in a week-long training session with them is to climb a 30-foot pole and leap off the top to catch a trapeze (supported by safety lines, of course). One group of managers included a wheelchair-bound paraplegic who wanted very much to take part in all the activities. The beliefs and assumptions (vapor wall) of many said that he could not be part of the pole exercise. He pushed, and the trainers huddled, and between them they found a solution. He climbed the pole, using the strength of his arms and the support of safety lines and his team shouting from below. When he reached the top he cried—and so did we.

—Former trainer with SportsMind

The wheelchair barrier turned out to be vapor. That participant and the trainers who worked with him found a way around the obstacles. When it was over, he said that he would never again feel constrained by the rules.

TO DO . . .

✓ The next time your employees question you about the rules (about their jobs, the organization or the work at hand), stop before you say, "It can't be done."
✓ Check to see which wall is holding you (and others?) in the box.
✓ Unless it is truly the concrete wall, work with your employee to bend or break the rules. Test the vapor wall and the beliefs that box you in. Evaluate new ideas fairly before you discard them.

Please Hold Your Questions Until the End

How many times have you heard that? Usually there is no time for the questions. Or the speaker didn't really want questions. If you are a question-friendly manager, you welcome employee questions and innovative thoughts at any time, in any amount and on any topic.

Alas

He was always too busy and we knew we shouldn't bother him with questions or new ideas about our processes. He liked to work by the book and he wanted us to follow the rules and just get it done. The sad thing was, our team came up with a better, faster way to turn out a superior product. We knew that if they were ever given a chance, our ideas could make money for the company. We kept our mouths shut and just kept working. I left the company and found a more innovative place to work.

—Supervisor, manufacturing team

Imagine the talent that is lost (often to the competitor) because no one took the time to listen to the challenging questions of innovative people.

Too Much of a Good Thing:
Rules, Guidelines, Policies, Procedures

All are necessary to some degree, especially to effectively operate large, complex organizations. But the rules often take on a life of their own. They multiply, they live in huge manuals, and they begin to stifle productivity and creativity. One team jokingly called themselves a "ship of rules."

Serena: Did you know that this approval form to spend $30 came back to me after three weeks in the organization with 15 signatures, including the CFO's?

Boss: Why on earth would it take all of that ridiculous time and effort?

Serena: It's the rule.

Boss: Let's see what we can do to break that one!

Reengineering (a process widely used in the 90s) was all about tearing down those restrictive rules. Many organizations literally started with a blank sheet of paper and created brand new processes, usually with fewer rules and steps. One hospital pulled all its employees into a large meeting room to examine the way they were doing the work. They had a mock patient enter their system. She and her paperwork moved around the room and met with people representing admissions, diagnosis, referral and treatment. Every stop represented the accepted rule and step for either the patient or her paperwork. The exercise revealed (to the horror of everyone) that one patient and her paperwork had made 50 stops through a bureaucratic maze before she began treatment.

Overgrown rules sometimes need questioning. If your talented employees get bogged down in them, they will spend too much time navigating the bureaucracy, not to mention filling out paperwork. They will spend too little time innovating and creating new solutions, services or products. They will also look for an opportunity to work elsewhere, in a freer workplace with fewer rules and restrictions.

see SPACE

TO DO . . .

✓ Encourage your employees' questions. Let them know that *any* time is a good time to ask.

✓ Support your employees' attempts to reduce the *number* of rules in your organization.

✓ Hold regular rule-busting meetings just to look at rules, systems and procedures that no longer work. Put different employees in charge of each meeting.

BOTTOM LINE

How long has it been since you have questioned the rules? And how much do you encourage questioning? Allow your employees to ask about the way work gets done and about the rules that help or hinder their productivity and satisfaction. By supporting their questioning you will greatly increase the odds of keeping your talent.

Chapter 18

REWARD

Provide Recognition

It wasn't about the money, really. Oh, sure, a bonus would have been nice when I brought that new client in, or when I finished those specs ahead of schedule. But even a "good going" would have been appreciated.

—A.J.

So this is the chapter about money, right? If not, where is that chapter? Isn't money a major motivator and a key reason people stay in their jobs?

Our competitors all pay 10 to 20 percent more for identical work. They come after us year after year, trying to steal us away from our organization. A few of us have been enticed away. While I would definitely appreciate a raise, I would not leave just to get one. The reason is that I feel rewarded in many other, less tangible ways. I'm rewarded by the actual work I do and by the appreciation my boss always shows. He has told me many times how critical I am to the success of the team. He is caring and finds creative ways to recognize our efforts. I feel important and valued.

—Supervisor, entertainment company

Decades of research and common sense tell you to pay fairly or your best people might leave. Benchmark similar organizations in your industry and find out what the pay scales, bonuses and perks look like. If you find that your compensation system is out of whack with your competitors', be concerned. Take your findings to your boss or to the compensation expert in your company and try to get things changed.

Pay fairly and pay competitively. But don't stop there. The research that suggests you need to pay fairly to keep your people also says that money alone won't keep them on your team. It is *not* the major motivator. Challenge, growth opportunities, flexibility, meaningful work, a good boss and recognition (often in nonmonetary forms) are examples of things that matter more to most of your people. When those are missing, talented people walk.

Rewarding Rules

Rule #1: *If an employee expects it, it may no longer be viewed as a reward.*

Alas

Every year I received a bonus, some stock options and a raise. I was hitting all the targets and doing a good job. It's funny how I left every one of those annual reviews feeling empty. The reward I wanted most was positive feedback from my boss. I wanted him to say that he really appreciated me and my contributions to the business. I really never felt recognized. That was a primary reason I left the company for another job.
—Manager, automobile manufacturer

You may think that the annual incentive bonus is ample reward and recognition for work well done. Your employee may see it differently. Company cars, cell phones, financial planning services and great health care plans are examples of company perks that many employees now expect as part of the package. They are no longer useful as special reward or recognition tools.

Rule #2: *Rewards need to match your employees' needs and wants.* How would you like to be recognized? We asked dozens of people this question and the following list represents some of what we heard. Notice the differences.

TO DO . . .

Check which forms of recognition you might appreciate. Also note which ones might *not* matter to you.

- ❏ An award, preferably given in front of my peers
- ❏ A plaque to hang on my wall
- ❏ A thank you, in writing, from my boss
- ❏ A note to my boss's boss about my excellent performance
- ❏ Frequent pats on the back
- ❏ My boss actually implementing one of my ideas
- ❏ A chance to be on a really exciting, cutting-edge project
- ❏ A bonus of some sort
- ❏ A day off
- ❏ Words of praise in front of my family
- ❏ A raise
- ❏ A chance to go to lunch with senior management
- ❏ Opportunity to work with people from other parts of the company
- ❏ A chance to be on one of the important steering committees
- ❏ A promotion
- ❏ A change in my title
- ❏ A small memento or gift
- ❏ Some flexibility in my schedule
- ❏ More freedom or autonomy

Many managers wrongly assume that everyone likes or wants the same types of rewards and recognition.

> *I will never forget the thrill of receiving an Excellence Award at the annual company conference. Seven hundred of my peers were there. My name was called and was written in huge letters across a massive screen. As I walked forward, it truly felt like an Academy Award moment—almost surreal. There was a cash prize that accompanied a beautiful glass trophy with my name inscribed on it. I had my picture taken with senior management.*
>
> *The cash was spent within weeks. But the trophy still sits on my desk, and the memory of that amazing moment of recognition will last a lifetime. I have never felt more appreciated or rewarded.*
>
> —Vice President, major consulting firm

see ASK

While this person was fully rewarded by all the hoopla at the conference, someone else might have been embarrassed or would have much preferred some other form of recognition. *Ask your employees what kind of recognition or reward they most appreciate.*

The Universal Reward

Praise works for everyone. There's really no such thing as too much praise (as long as it's sincere). Regardless of individual differences, virtually all employees want to hear how valuable they are to the team, how important their work is, and what great work they have done. And they are happy to hear it again and again.

> *He used to stop me in the hall, just to ask how things were going. Then he would say, "Tom, we couldn't do without you. You oughta be the CFO." I was just an accountant, but he made me feel so important to the organization. I'd head back to my office pumped up and ready to go!*
>
> —Accountant, aerospace firm

Ken Blanchard's famous book, *The One Minute Manager*[1], reminds managers to praise their employees. We suggest you take your employees' individual preferences into account and then do the following:

TO DO . . .

Praise your employees:

✓ *Spontaneously.* Catch people doing something right and thank them then and there. (Thank you, Ken Blanchard!)
✓ *Specifically.* Praise people for *specific* (rather than generic) accomplishments or efforts.
✓ *Purposefully.* Take an employee to lunch or dinner in a great restaurant to show your appreciation of work well done.
✓ *Privately.* Go to your employee's office to give a personal thank-you and praise.
✓ *Publicly.* Praise an employee in the presence of others (peers, family members, your boss).
✓ *In writing.* Send a letter, memo or e-mail. Possibly send a copy to team members or higher-level management.

Compensation is a right; recognition is a gift.
—Rosabeth Moss Kanter, author and management consultant

Get Out of the Box

As you struggle to think of other creative ways to reward and recognize your employees, try this. Think about yourself. What could your boss do that would really demonstrate how much he or she values you (besides giving you a raise or praise)? Remembering individual differences, you can use your own list to begin thinking about how to reward your employees. Here are a few hints that will get you started.

Time

What a precious commodity. Give an outstanding employee the afternoon off. Let another sleep late. Thank a whole team by giving them a Friday off. Let them decide *when* to use their gift of time.

> One boss created a days-off bank. He put 25 days in the bank and then used those days to reward individuals and teams for outstanding performance.

Toys

What toys might they want? A cappuccino machine? A dart board in the lounge? A volleyball court between buildings? Tickets to the movies?

> The way we see it, spending one dollar on something clever and unique is better than spending 50 dollars on something ordinary and forgettable.
>
> —Richard File, Partner, Amrigon

Trophies and Trinkets

What small mementos or trophies would be meaningful? It could be a customized plaque, a coffee cup with a personal thank you note inscribed, or a refrigerator magnet with the perfect message.

> Simple observation suggests that most of us are trinket freaks—if they represent a genuine thanks for a genuine assist.
>
> —Tom Peters, author and management consultant

> The Gumby award became treasured. It all started when one employee showed phenomenal flexibility in helping teammates deliver a project on time. He showed up at work the next day to find a giant Gumby doll sitting in his chair. It probably cost five dollars, but that trophy became the most sought-after prize in the organization and people were elated when it showed up in their offices.
>
> —Consultant, transition consulting firm

Opportunity

What opportunities might your employees want? The chance to be part of a steering committee or to give a presentation to the senior team? A chance to ride in the company jet or visit another plant? Choice about the next project or a chance to learn something new?

- ✓ One boss paid for a training class (of the person's choosing) to be taken on company time.
- ✓ Another showed appreciation by allowing an employee to "shadow" someone else in order to learn new skills.
- ✓ Still another boss gave the opportunity to deliver a critical presentation to senior management.

see OPPORTUNITIES

Fun

How about an outing on company time? Leaving work early to play ball or take a hike together? Playing hooky together and going to a movie? Having a spontaneous pizza party in the office some afternoon?

> *The team had been working long hours and even weekends. The boss suggested that we rent a limousine, buy some great food and wine and go to an outdoor concert. He picked up the tab. We felt so pampered and rewarded for all the effort and our outstanding results.*
> —Vice President, compensation firm

see KICKS

Freedom

What kind of freedom might they want? Flextime? Freedom to work from home, to dress casually, to change the way they do some of the work? Freedom to work without supervision? Freedom to manage a budget?

> *One manager rewarded his secretary by giving her a monthly budget of $400 to use as she saw fit. She could buy office supplies, order lunch for the department, etc. It showed that the boss appreciated and trusted her.*

see SPACE

Small Money

Sometimes it's a small sum ($50–100) to put toward whatever the rewarded employee wants. This discretionary, on-the-spot cash award is sometimes more deeply appreciated than one might ever guess.

> *Alan was so proud. He completed a set of last minute specs, stayed late, and in general went above and beyond. To thank him, his boss gave him a $150 check and told him to spend it on a "toy" ASAP. Alan bought one of those miniature airball tables and proudly brought it home. His kids were excited and when they asked why the gift, he answered, "It's not a gift for you. It's for me, from my company, for doing a great job." The kids were impressed. Four years later the toy is still in use in the family room. When anyone says to his kids, "How cool," they say, "Our dad got it for his good work." Alan smiles every time.*

Big Money

Peter Cappelli, chairman of the management department at the Wharton School of Business, says that higher wages are not necessarily the principal way to lure good workers any more. Yet it may be exactly what some people want. Find out who of your talented employees is truly motivated by money. See what you can do for them. Would a bonus for exceeding goals and expectations help? A larger raise than expected? Think about where you can stretch your budget to reward with money when it is warranted and *desired*. If your hands are tied because you know for a fact that more dollars are an impossibility, here's one more option. Tell them the truth! Then inquire (and we admit it may not be easy) what else your employee might want other than dollars. At first this may be uncomfortable for both of you. If you hang in there, however, we think other alternatives will appear. And if you can keep brainstorming long enough, one or more of those options may just be other currencies you can trade on. The key is that you let employees know how much you value them and their contributions.

TO DO . . .

✓ Take an honest look at how you reward and recognize your employees. How do you know that it is effective?
✓ Ask people what matters most to them.
✓ Reward according to individual needs and wants.
✓ Remember to praise generously and genuinely. *It works for everyone!*

BOTTOM LINE

Over and over, research has told us that money is not the major key to keeping good people. We double checked this research with our own, and it proved true. When employees across the country answered the question, "What kept you?" no group had dollars in the top five reasons. Money will not guarantee that your talent stays. People want recognition for work well done. Assess your pay scale to be sure it's fair. Then *praise your good people.* Find creative ways to show your appreciation, and you will increase the odds of keeping them.

Chapter 19

 **S**PACE

Give It

My boss gave me no space to think or create or even manage my own time. I felt controlled and hemmed in with no room to grow.

—A.J.

Anyone who has raised a teenager (or remembers being one) knows the phrase *give me some space*! It is commonly uttered by someone who feels fenced in, overcontrolled or frustrated by his lack of power over his own situation. Dilbert, the cartoon spokesperson for corporate American office workers, constantly profiles managers as control freaks who give their employees little or no space, either physically (as in cubicle dwellers) or figuratively (as in space to control one's own day-to-day existence).

Think about the last boss you had who dictated your every move, gave you no freedom, held stringently to the policy manual, or was never open to new ways of doing anything. How long did you stay in that job? (Hope you are not there now!) That boss didn't understand inner space or outer space, and employees will leave if they don't have enough of both.

Inner and Outer Space

By *inner space* we mean the space your employees want and need mentally and emotionally in order to feel like creative, productive, thinking members of the team. It includes space to:

✓ Be self-directed
✓ Manage one's own time
✓ Work and think in new ways

As a manager, you can give your talented employees the inner space they want (it usually costs you nothing) and increase the odds that they will stay on your team.

Outer space refers to the physical world and primarily to employees' work environment. It includes space to:

✓ Design one's own work area
✓ Work from different places
✓ Take a break
✓ Dress as one wishes

Managing your employees' outer space requests might require some stepping out of the box behaviors for you, especially if your organization has never done it that way. Before we tell you what some other managers are doing to give more space, take this short quiz to determine your own space-giving tendencies. Keep score.

see QUESTION

TO DO . . .

Read the following scenarios, imagining that you are the boss of this team, and think about your responses to their requests. Decide when you would say yes or no, and why. Use the answer box that follows.

1. I want to adjust my work schedule (for personal reasons) three days a week, to come in half an hour earlier and leave half an hour earlier.

2. I want to get this task done in a brand new way, not like you have seen it done before.

3. I want to complete the first five steps of this project before I have you review it with me.

4. I want to try a new technique, one that I am more comfortable with, to increase sales.

5. Instead of taking that class you recommended, I found a mentor I want to learn that skill from.

6. I just took some great pictures on my vacation and want to put them on my office/cubicle walls.

7. I want to work from home two days a week.

8. I plan to work on Saturdays for a few weeks in order to get a project done on time. I want to bring my well-trained dog to work with me on those days.

9. I want to wear casual clothes to work, rather than a business suit. I am much more comfortable and creative in my jeans and tennis shoes.

10. I know we've always done these projects solo, but I want to put together a team this time because I believe we will do a better job, more quickly.

11. I want six weeks off work (without pay) to begin the building of my own home.

12. I want to bring my new baby to work for the first six weeks of her life.

Answer Box

Your Response	1	2	3	4	5	6	7	8	9	10	11	12
Sure, no problem.												
No way.												
Let me see what I can do.												

The list of requests you just considered will give you a clue about the kind of space-giving we are talking about. The first five have more to do with Inner Space, and the remaining seven relate to Outer Space.

1. Count the number of scenarios where you said, "Sure, no problem, as long as you get the job done."
2. Now count the number where you said, "No way," "It's never been done that way," or "Our policy manual forbids that."
3. Finally, how about the number of times you said, "Let me see what I can do for you. I will need to take this to my boss," or "Tell me more about what you need and I'll see what I can do."

How Did You Score?

Sure, no problem.	8 or higher	You are *space friendly*. Keep doing what works!
No way.	3 or more	You are *space unfriendly*. Try the "let me see" phrase next time!
Let me see what I can do.	Any number	You are *space aware*. Your employees will appreciate your efforts!

In some organizations every one of these requests would be met with a positive response, but the opposite is true in far too many. Would you be surprised to know that those organizations are not on anyone's preferred employer list, and that they are having greater difficulty recruiting and retaining their employees? We believe that no matter how well these organizations pay, they will ultimately lose their talented people, simply because they do not give them *space!* So how can you give employees the space they need?

Giving Outer Space

Space to Work from Different Places

One of the most frequent ways managers are giving employees their space is by allowing telecommuting. According to a survey conducted by

Telecommute America, more than 11 million people currently work from home or remote offices daily. That's quite a few people putting a lot of distance between themselves and their bosses, yet it seems to be working. Nancy Kurland, assistant professor of management and organizations at The University of Southern California's Marshall School of Business, said, "Telecommuters tend to work longer hours because they feel telecommuting is a privilege and they want to make sure it's not taken away."[1]

What if your organization does not allow it?

My company had never allowed telecommuting and I believed it probably never would. One of my top employees asked me if she could work from home two days a week and my immediate response was no. A month later she sadly handed in her resignation and said she had found an employer who would allow her to telecommute. I simply could not afford to lose her, so I went to my boss and asked if we might bend the rules on a trial basis, offer her telecommuting two days a week and see how productive she was. She stayed with us, increased her actual productivity by 10 percent and is a grateful, loyal employee. Since then we have loosened our policy considerably and consider telecommuting on a case by case basis for any employee who requests it.

—Accounting manager, city government

Some jobs simply must be performed at the work site and telecommuting will never be an option. When that is the case, think about other ways that you can give your employees space.

Sometimes the organization has no rule about working from another place, but the manager says no anyway. If you are one of those managers, ask yourself why. Is it a lack of trust in your employees? Is it concern that they will "goof off" or not be productive without your ever-vigilant eye? If that is the case, consider managing based on results. Be clear about your expectations: what do you want them to produce or create? By when? Consider letting your employees get those results from whatever location they wish.

Alas

I think of myself as cutting edge in many ways. But in other ways I think I'm stuck in old paradigms and bound by old rules. I've lost three key employees in the past year. Each one wanted something I couldn't give (or thought I couldn't)—like a chance to to telecommute two days a week or casual dress. Recently I saw another manager work out a deal with one of her prized employees. She got permission for him to work very different hours from everyone else. He's thrilled and producing like crazy. Now I'm rethinking my tendency to immediately say no to requests coming my way. Maybe I need to flex more in order to keep the talent on my team.

—Manager, hotel chain

Space to Take a Break

A talented young engineer in a large aerospace firm asked his immediate boss for six weeks off work (without pay), to begin building his house. His boss said okay, even though the engineer's absence would certainly be a hardship. After the six weeks, the engineer came back to his boss, asking for an additional four weeks, as he just hadn't done as much as he had hoped on his house. The boss pondered the request, thought about how valued this employee was, ran the request up the ladder to the division engineer and came back with the okay. The engineer remained a loyal, committed employee for another 24 years. He later became a member of the senior management team and helped lead his company to tremendous success. When asked what he would have done had they turned down his request, he said he would have quit the job and found a new one after completing his project.

Seldom do we find managers who value their employees enough to allow them the space to truly take a break from work. Yet, in some countries and in certain fields (such as college teaching), sabbaticals are actually encouraged. Valuable employees are supported in their decisions to travel or learn something new or simply go to the mountains and meditate. The next time your talented employee asks you for a break, consider the pros and cons and get creative about finding a way to make it happen. Your employee will feel supported and the odds of your retaining that talent for the future will go up.

Space to Dress How One Wishes

We have all read about the high-tech environment where people with creative, brilliant minds dress in all kinds of bizarre outfits. Some wonder if it is appropriate or professional or conducive to productivity. The results seem to speak for themselves. Just take a look at Microsoft or Netscape, where there are *no dress codes* in many departments. How successful and productive have they been over the years? Managers in those environments say that their employees often work long hours (sometimes 70-hour weeks) by their own choosing, as they strive to complete a project or get a new product out the door. Allowing them to dress as they wish seems a small concession, considering the commitment and high level of productivity.

> *I don't feel I need to dress up to meet an equation.*
>
> —Aerospace engineer

Think about where you can offer flexibility in dress. Is it the Friday casual day or summer attire or different dress codes for those who never see a customer? Challenge the rules a bit. Are they reasonable, or not? If business wear is truly necessary, then you will clearly want to support the rule—but think about the requirements realistically and with a creative eye. It is truly amazing how favorably many employees view a flexible dress code.

Should all work areas in your organization look alike? Anyone who has studied personality differences knows that one way we express our uniqueness is in our surroundings. Our homes, our offices and yes, our cubicles, will reflect our preferences and our style, if we are given the freedom to do with those spaces what we wish.

Many organizations today hire interior decorating firms that design beautiful, perfect work areas. In some of those workplaces, the decorating rules are quite explicit and there is no room for personalization at all. What about your organization? If the rules allow for some flexibility, then you as a manager have *room to allow space* for your employees. Let them bring in their favorite pictures and organize (or not) their desks the way they wish. Do not demand that everyone have work spaces like yours.

At Apple, one worker, a very visual thinker, was stunted when he was forced to sit at his computer to put down his thoughts. To help facilitate his thinking, his manager covered all the walls of his office with dry-erase board.

*****

To give employees their space, Netscape allows them to set their own hours, dress however they want and furnish their space any way they want. As a result some employees have sofas, refrigerators, stereos and even fish tanks.

Giving Inner Space

Space to Be Self-Directed and to Work and Think in New Ways

Giving inner space requires that managers *let go and trust* their talented employees to manage their work effectively and to continuously improve their work.

The retail giant Nordstrom knows a lot about giving its employees space and empowering them to make decisions and manage their own work. In fact, managers believe that it is precisely due to their corporate culture that they have one of the highest retention rates in the retail industry. The primary rule, stated in Nordstrom's Employee Handbook, is: Use your good judgment at all times.

Because workers are empowered to do anything they can to make sure the customer is satisfied, Nordstrom customers typically experience remarkable service. The employee who ironed the new shirt a customer needed for a meeting and the one who gift-wrapped items a customer had bought at Macy's are both examples of how Nordstrom employees provide great customer service. They are given the space to manage their work in their own unique and creative way.

A five-year veteran employee with a record of superior customer service summed it up this way, "Where else could I get paid so well and have so much autonomy? Nordstrom is one of the first places I've ever felt like I really belong to something special. Sure I work really hard, but I like to work hard. No one tells me what to do, and I feel I can go as far as my dedication will take me. I feel like an entrepreneur."[2]

A pilot from Southwest Airlines and an accountant at Microsoft both relate similar stories of flexible environments with a minimum of bureaucracy and almost no micromanagement. Even though the jobs and the companies are very different, both employees feel truly fortunate to have such a high level of control over their work. Although the pilot certainly has very strict schedules to meet and clearly defined safety rules, he feels that his boss and the Southwest culture as a whole give him tremendous personal flexibility. The Microsoft accountant describes an environment that is typical in high-tech companies, where talent is hard to find and harder to keep. Employees' hours, physical space, dress, and *even the way they approach their tasks* are left up to each individual or team.

TO DO . . .

✓ Let your employees manage more aspects of their own work, without direct supervision.

✓ Trust them to get it right and then assist when they need your help.

✓ Allow them to try new ways of accomplishing the tasks at hand even if "it's never been done that way before!"

You probably have more space as a manager to *give space to your employees* in this arena than in any other, and the payoff is tremendous. If you cannot offer telecommuting or casual dress codes, you *can* offer the power to manage the way they do the day-to-day work.

Space to Manage One's Own Time

This may be another area where you say, "I have no control. We have strict policies about work hours and how/where they are spent." If that is true, then you will want to consider other ways of offering space to your employees. We encourage you, however, to test the rules a bit and see where there might be some flexibility to offer your employees space to manage their work time according to their own unique needs. Here are some creative ways in which managers are looking at flexible work schedules and allowing employees to truly manage their own time:

At both Merck and Hewlett-Packard, employees work five days a week, eight hours a day. These companies' version of flextime gives employees a two-hour window in which to begin work in the morning and a two-hour window in which to stop for the day and go home.

*****

At Federal Express, workers are allowed to arrive ten minutes before their shift begins and leave ten minutes earlier or vice versa. This ten-minute window can substantially reduce driving time during rush hours, making a huge difference in an employee's stress level. (Sometimes a shift of just ten minutes in a work schedule can make the difference.)

*****

Ernst & Young has opened—for its own use—a nationwide database of employees who have untraditional schedules. It profiles people and their tasks, how the individuals worked things out with their supervisors, and the results. Any employee can use it to find a role model, from the partners on down. The program of trumpeting flexible schedules has been such a hit that almost 1,000 people out of a national workforce of 29,000 are currently on a flexible schedule.

Retention of women senior managers in Ernst & Young's largest practice rose 7 percent in 18 months, while revenues increased more than 20 percent. Meanwhile people working flexible schedules were promoted at exactly the same rate as the 9 to 5 crowd.[3]

BOTTOM LINE

Job sharing, flextime, telecommuting and designing one's own work space. What we're really talking about is listening to what people want, going to bat for their needs, and ultimately giving them options and opportunities to do things differently. Truly listen to the unique and diverse requests that employees bring you. Make small concessions and bend the rules where you can. Run requests up the flagpole in the honest attempt to win flexibility and improved work conditions for your people.

Space to play, have a good time, take breaks, celebrate successes, creatively attack problems—all of this makes for a retention culture. The reward for you will be loyalty and commitment from your best people. They will stick around and perform.

 **TRUTH**

Tell It

I can handle the truth. Why couldn't they just tell me?

—A.J.

Are you an honest person? Do you believe in telling the truth? Most people will say yes to both questions. But think of how many times you've told someone, "You look terrific!" when you didn't mean it. As adults we know that honesty is the best policy, but that doesn't mean we always tell the truth.

Our studies show that employees yearn for straight talk. They want to *hear* the truth about their performance and the organization. They want to *tell you* the truth about *your* performance. When they feel they're not hearing or telling the truth, they may suffer lower morale, lack of confidence in their leaders and ultimately loss of loyalty to the organization. Of course you know where that might lead—right out your door and into the competition's. Tell the truth if you want to keep your good people.

A New View of Truth-Telling

The secret of truth-telling is to view it as a *gift*. If you believe that giving truthful, balanced feedback to people will truly help them to be more effective in their careers (maybe in life as a whole), then you will be more inclined to give that feedback. Have you ever taken music or dance lessons, had a baseball, tennis or golf coach? Think back to that time and recall one of your sessions with that person.

Did he demonstrate a better way to grip the racket or club? Did she help you develop better rhythm or tone with your instrument? Weren't they constantly helping you to fine-tune your approach to the sport or the skill? The feedback was probably balanced between *praise*—"That was great, play it again just like that!"—and *correction*—"This time hold the bat more like this." Their job was often to hold up a mirror for you so that you could see exactly what you were doing. Sometimes you performed in front of a mirror or were even videotaped. Their gift was honest feedback, from someone willing to tell you there was still room for improvement and committed to helping you get there. Your employees expect and need the same kind of coaching from you today.

Tell Them the Truth About Their Work

Think about the people who work with you or report to you. Think about their relative strengths and weaknesses, their blind spots, their overused strengths, and the flaws that may stall or stop them as they attempt to progress in their careers. Have you been honest and direct with these people about your perceptions?

When and how did you give them your input? Even the "best bosses" might honestly confess that they have trouble giving people direct feedback, especially about possible flaws or areas where they need improvement. These managers may be concerned about hurting their employees' feelings, turning them off, demoralizing them, or even prompting someone to quit because of negative feedback.

Alas

I honestly thought I was doing a great job. I had been promoted several times, had positive performance reviews and got a bonus every year. The next thing I knew I was passed over for a big promotion, shoved in a corner and ignored. When the downsizing happened, I was laid off. Only then did I hear that there had been some problems with my management style through the years.

—Unemployed middle manager

Most of us were not trained to give negative news. Our elders taught us that "honesty is the best policy," but we also learned, "If you can't say something nice, don't say anything at all." So, we don't.

The Truth Hurts, or Does It?

When employees in most organizations are asked what they would like more of from their managers, their first response is usually *feedback*. People want to know where they stand—they want to know if your perception of their performance is the same as their own. They want the truth.

Years of research (much of it done at the Center for Creative Leadership) confirms that the lack of honest feedback is a major cause of derailment for leaders at all levels. Derailment sometimes means getting fired, but more often it means failing to achieve what a person was seen as capable of.[1] Even the "stars" in your organization need honest, balanced feedback. Too often they hear only how wonderful, bright and talented they are. Lack of feedback can cause these employees to derail and come to a startling, shocking halt after several promotions, big raises and starring roles. Why? Because no one helped them see their rough edges and the need for continual improvement. They began to believe their own press clippings and developed major blind spots. Their confidence slowly but surely turned into arrogance, in part because of insufficient, inaccurate, imbalanced or tardy feedback from bosses and other key people in their lives. The truth could have saved them.

TO DO . . .

✓ Within the next 30 days, give honest feedback to all of your employees, the high performers and solid citizens alike. They deserve it and will appreciate your giving it to them.

But I Already Gave Feedback—In December

In many organizations managers are only required to give feedback during the annual performance review. They give input to reward and reinforce employees' behaviors and performance, to justify the annual raise or to warn them about unsatisfactory performance and possible consequences. Some managers gloss over the negatives and focus on the good news only, and others do just the opposite. In either case, employees are often left frustrated by the whole process.

Two points:

1. The formal performance appraisal meeting is important and can be very valuable for your employees. If it is handled badly, your employees may feel disrespected and unimportant. Plan carefully and tell them the truth at these meetings. Balance the *good news* (positive) with the *important news* (room for improvement).

2. Don't give feedback just once a year. To retain your key people it is essential that you give regular, honest feedback on an ongoing basis.

Alas

In our organization, the employee and boss both fill out the performance appraisal form once a year. The idea is to compare results and have a discussion about the employee's performance and where he might improve. I spent hours filling mine out, really trying to evaluate my strengths and weaknesses and how I had done on my goals. I turned it in to my boss three weeks before our "big meeting." When I showed up, it became clear that he had not looked at my report at all and had filled in his form in a hurry, minutes before the meeting. All the ratings were just average, and when I asked him how I could bring them up, he said he would have to think about it. Twenty minutes later he said he had another meeting. So—I had waited all year to get feedback from my boss, and when it finally came, it was mediocre and almost meaningless. I have never felt so insignificant—maybe I need to start looking around for another job.

—Nursing supervisor, hospital

What If I Don't Know How?

Many managers are uncomfortable giving feedback, either positive or negative, because they don't know how to do it simply and effectively. Many have never had a good role model. Giving feedback so that it can be heard nondefensively is key. How do you measure up? Take this true-false quiz to see if you are feedback-savvy.

Feedback Quiz
My feedback . . .

✓ Is private. (I choose a place where the person can hear my comments without being distracted or embarrassed.)
_____ True _____ False

✓ Receives the time it deserves. (I plan the time and use it just for the purpose of giving feedback to someone.)
_____ True   _____ False

✓ Is frequent. (I give feedback immediately after actions that need changing or rewarding.)
_____ True   _____ False

✓ Focuses more on the future than the past. (I talk mostly about what can be done to improve, rather than what went wrong.)
_____ True   _____ False

✓ Is specific, with clear examples. ("I think you need to delegate more. You did all of last quarter's project yourself.")
_____ True   _____ False

✓ Gives information that helps the person to make decisions. ("Your team wants you to involve them more in planning.")
_____ True   _____ False

✓ Gives suggestions for growth and improvement. ("I think you could work on negotiating skills, especially if you want that new role.")
_____ True   _____ False

✓ Allows for discussion. ("Tell me what you are thinking. What do you want to do about this?")
_____ True   _____ False

✓ Creates next steps. ("Let's meet again next week to create a development plan for you. Meanwhile, think about what you'd like to include in that plan.")
_____ True   _____ False

How did you do? If most of these statements are true for you, fantastic! Now go ask your employees if they agree. Ask them to tell you the truth.

Confidentially Speaking . . .

Another approach that is gaining in popularity in many corporations large and small is 360-degree feedback. In this approach, your employees receive feedback from you, their peers, customers and direct reports.

That feedback is very specific and is about their competencies (skills, behaviors, attitudes and traits). It highlights both strengths and opportunities to improve and its purpose is *developmental*. Because it is usually anonymous, raters tend to be very honest. It is often important and valuable for your employees (you too) to get input from someone other than the boss; 360-degree feedback is just one way of doing that.

TO DO . . .

✓ If you have an employee who is having difficulty understanding or believing that he has weaknesses, or who has blind spots that you just cannot seem to penetrate, you might consider getting input for him from others via a 360-degree feedback tool. Your human resources professional should be able to help you choose the right approach and the most appropriate tool.

Tell Them the Truth About the Organization

Research overwhelmingly supports the notion that satisfied employees are "in the know." They want to be trusted with the truth about the business, including its challenges and downturns. Managers who trust their employees with the truth are trusted, in turn, by their employees. It's a powerful, positive cycle.

see INFORMATION

We know, however, that there may be times when you are simply not at liberty to tell the whole truth. You may have been given information that you are simply not supposed to share with subordinates. A pending merger, reorganization or change at the top of the organization could be off-limits for discussion with your team.

But sometimes managers hold information back in the belief that it makes them somehow more powerful or that it is better for their employees not to know. We know that it's especially difficult when the truth is bad news. In this situation, give it directly, face to face and as soon as possible. If you have made a mistake, confess, tell them the truth and accept responsibility. Your personal stock will go up and so will the trust level on your team.

Ask Them for the Truth (Even About You)

We would rather be ruined by praise then saved by criticism.
—Norman Vincent Peale

So far we've been talking about telling the truth to your employees. But what about getting them to tell you the truth? Many managers (especially at high levels) have had no formal performance reviews or feedback sessions for years. By the time they rise to the top, they might be getting almost no balanced, accurate input, especially about *how* they get the work done. Often, as long as the bottom-line targets are hit, leaders are rewarded.

Who then tells the senior leader about his warts? Probably no one. That oversight and the absence of truthful, balanced feedback creates leaders who have missed the opportunity to grow, to be even more effective in their jobs and to keep their talented people.

In almost every setting outside the modern American organization, the experts and masters continue to ask for the truth about their performance and they strive for improvement. Athletes, musicians and martial arts masters are examples of this. *You* can establish an environment where truth is welcome. And you can serve as a model for your employees as they watch how *you seek and receive* feedback. Do your best to view it as a gift.

Even people who don't mind telling the truth have mixed feelings about hearing the truth. It's like a chemical reaction: Your face goes red, your temperature rises, you want to strike back. Those are signs of the two D's: Defending and Debating. Try to fight back with the two L's: Listening and Learning.

—Jerry Hirshberg[2]

BOTTOM LINE

Telling the truth is a healthy philosophy both personally and professionally. People who are trusted to hear the truth about themselves and the organization, and to tell the truth about you, are more satisfied and more loyal. Loyal, happy employees are the ones who stick around.

Chapter 21

UNDERSTAND

Listen Deeper

My boss never really understood me.

—A.J.

"You're not listening. You *never* listen." If you ever hear these complaints, at home or at work, read on. Why is there no end to the training courses on this subject? Why do feedback surveys repeatedly tell managers that they are lousy listeners? Why don't we *get it*?

Most managers don't really believe that listening is a critical skill. They believe that being results-oriented or customer-focused is much more important to business success than being a good listener. Are they right?

Joe understands me. He listens to me—and I feel understood. The more he listens, the more I reveal and the stronger our relationship becomes. We have developed a huge amount of trust. With other bosses, I used to edit. I tell him everything. As a result, he is never surprised. He has a better handle on things. Because of our bond we are more creative, take bigger risks, push the boundaries and accomplish amazing things. I have never had a better boss and I have never been so productive. Right now, nothing could entice me away from this job.

—Senior vice president, engineering organization

Our research has continually affirmed our belief that an unsatisfactory work relationship with their manager is one of the major reasons people leave. Articles in many newsletters and magazines suggest this is true even in the post-loyalty culture.

see BUCK

TO DO . . .

✓ Stop now and write down three or four things you learned from your employees this week. It could be a process improvement idea, a customer challenge or a team issue. If you can't list three or four, you probably have not been listening carefully enough to your employees.

Communication is critical to keeping your talent. If they feel heard, understood and valued by you, they will work harder and produce more. They will *want* to stay and work for you. And if they don't—they will leave.

Tune Out—Miss Out

The manager's head moves up and down. She says, "Uh-huh," 35 times in a row. Is she listening? Probably not. So what gets in the way of listening deeper? What are you thinking about while your employee talks?

TO DO . . .

Which of these do you sometimes think while your employees talk to you? Be honest:

✓ I already know the punch line. I'm five steps ahead.
✓ I'm too busy for this. I have a stack of work on my desk.
✓ He's getting emotional. I'm checking out.
✓ I wonder how my son is doing in school today.
✓ Now, what should my response be? How can I defend my position?
✓ She's so boring. I'm going to plan my meeting while she talks.

How did you do? You might believe that it is great time management (multitasking) to have your mind busy while another person talks, or to be planning your response so that you are ready the minute the employee stops speaking. You might be impatient. You might believe that your time and ideas are worth more than your employee's. Or you may have just forgotten how to really focus on a person and listen deeply. Regardless of your reason, the result is the same. When you *tune out*, you *miss out*. You miss out on information. More importantly, you miss out on having a respectful relationship with that individual.

Listening Is a Choice

You might already have great listening skills and habits, but you are selective about when you use them. Be conscious about how you are listening to your employees. Decide to listen deeper. Truly try to understand your talented people.

What stands out most, and what kept me at that company for many years, was really a simple thing. Every Friday we'd get together at a local pub and the general manager would come in and start the party with one question, "So, how was your week?" We'd all go on and on about the problems we had faced, the successes we'd had, the issues that we still had to deal with. We didn't really solve much (although that happened occasionally). Mostly we all just vented. And the amazing thing was, he was truly interested. We went home those weekends feeling great.

—Employee, furniture retail company

Listen Up, or Is It Down?

Listening experts talk about levels of listening. One of them, Madelyn Burley-Allen, explains that the two superficial levels are hearing words, but not really listening, and listening in spurts (tuning in and out). She describes *empathic* listening as the deepest level. It is nonjudging, focused on the speaker, and it leads to truly understanding the other person.[1]

Most of us spend little time in empathic, deep listening and aren't sure how to develop that skill. Here is one way.

The BLINKING Word

Many managers are becoming better listeners by learning a simple technique called the BLINKING word. Here is how it works.

Scenario: Your employee, Shelby, asks to talk to you, so you schedule a meeting in your office. You welcome Shelby in and ask what you can do for her. She says, "I'm having trouble with one of my employees. He seems to lack motivation for the job."

1. Identify the words that BLINK (stand out).

   *"I'm having **trouble** with one of my employees. He seems to **lack motivation** for the job."*

2. Ask about one of the BLINKING words.

   "What kind of trouble?" or "How does he seem to lack motivation?"

3. Listen for Shelby's answer.

   *"He's not as **productive** as he used to be."*

4. Notice the BLINKING word in her answer and question it.

   "How has his productivity dropped?"

5. Listen for Shelby's answer.

   *"He gets **less** work done in a week and the **quality** has **slipped** too."*

6. Notice the BLINKING word in her answer and question it.

   "Why do you think he is getting less work done?" or *"Tell me about the slip in quality."*

7. Keep going, watch for the BLINKING words and ask about them.

Use open questions as you follow the BLINKING words. Open questions begin with words like *how, why, where, when, tell me about.* By following the BLINKING word, you go deeper into Shelby's problem. Meanwhile, Shelby feels listened to. She believes that you care about her dilemma and are there to help her solve it. The BLINKING word technique will force you to listen empathetically, at the deepest level. You will not be able to tune in and out and still follow the BLINKING word. (P.S. *Do* try this at home. Your spouse, kids, friends will be pleasantly surprised at what a good listener you have become.)

Alas

I watched him read his mail while his employees talked to him. I was on the receiving end of that behavior a few times myself. He probably thought we didn't notice, or that we respected his ability to multitask. He was wrong. We felt unimportant and not heard *most of the time.*

—Front-line employee

Listening Liabilities

These deterrents to effective listening may prevent you from understanding your employees and, ultimately, from keeping them on your team.

The Interrupter

Have you ever tried to have a conversation with someone who finishes your sentences? Who interrupts with their own brilliant thought about the topic? Your employees will lose patience with you and may quit coming to you with their ideas and challenges if you interrupt them at every turn.

Notice when you interrupt your employees. Use the BLINKING word technique. Let them do the talking while you do the listening. Give them credit for great ideas and *let them finish*.

The Defender

Defensive listeners also interrupt. They may be defending their thinking, their stand on a topic, the status quo, or their status or role in the organization. Notice if you are a defender. Stop and let your employees explain their thinking or their position on a topic. Try to really understand them before you rush to your own defense.

The Transmitter

Some people seem to transmit only. They spend more time talking than listening. What percentage of the time are you typically talking: 20 percent, 80 percent? Someone once said that God gave us two ears and one mouth for a reason—we should be listening twice as much as we are talking. Try giving your employees a chance to say more.

Listen Deeper

Some managers wonder, "What should I be listening for?" We believe it is important to listen for:

✓ *Input.* Talented people want to have an ear for their great ideas and solutions. They want to be heard and recognized.

see REWARD

My boss not only listened to my ideas, but she let me present them at the board meeting. I felt so proud.

—Manager, real estate management firm

✓ *Motivations.* What do they want from this job and from you? What gets them up in the morning and looking forward to their work?

He asked me what I liked about the job and what I wasn't so thrilled with. He listened. Once he really understood where I was coming from, he suggested that we hand off some of my least favorite tasks to a colleague who likes doing that work. He seems to really understand me.

—Supervisor, medical group

✓ *Challenges.* You need to know about your employees' problems and challenges.

One of my direct reports has a talented employee named Denise. Her performance level had dropped and we were wondering why. I suggested that we both meet with her. We asked Denise if something was bothering her and she began to talk. Finally she shared that she was battling cancer but had been afraid to tell us. We listened to her for two hours. She said that she felt so much better now that the secret was out, and she thanked us for our support and understanding. That was two years ago. Denise has made it through the tough times and has recently been promoted.

—Director, advertising firm

Getting to Know Them

It's not too late to learn how to listen more effectively and learn more about the talented people you want to keep. Think of yourself as an archaeologist on a dig. Take your curiosity to the relationship and see what you can learn.

TO DO ...

✓ Invite employees you do not know well to have lunch with you. Ask about them and their interests. Practice listening.

✓ Accept style differences among your employees. Listen to your slow talkers as well as the fast ones.

✓ Listen and act on ideas your employees bring you. When they see that you have implemented one of their ideas, they will feel heard.

✓ Notice little things. Go to your employees' work spaces and take note of the family pictures or sports trophies. Ask about them.

✓ Open your door. One employee said, "Sometimes I'd walk into my boss's office stressed and uptight. He would say, 'What do you need, some listening time?' I always felt like he accepted me and understood me."

✓ Slow down and listen. Sometimes managers are just moving too quickly (mentally and physically) to get to know and understand their employees.

✓ Clear your desk so you can focus on your employee, not the latest report you need to read.

✓ Notice your employee's eye color. This will help you connect eye-to-eye with that person.

✓ Remember to use the BLINKING word technique to listen deeper.

BOTTOM LINE

Strive to understand your employees by really listening to them. Pay attention to your own listening style and improve it (there's always room). Your efforts will pay off. Employees who feel heard and understood will stay on your team. Those who don't will find another place to work, with a boss who *will* listen.

Chapter 22

VALUES

Define and Align

My manager's values never lined up with the organization's values, so my own values seemed irrelevant.

—A.J.

Understanding how employees' values align with organizational values is a critical ingredient in keeping your best people. Organizations have vision statements, mission statements and values statements, but they rarely have a process that helps employees determine the link between those and their own values. In fact, many employees have never examined their values in a formal way. They would have a difficult time responding if you asked a question like, "What are your values?" or more specifically, "What are your career-related values?" The risk of losing employees because of values conflicts is far greater than the risk of losing them because of compensation.

When your work is aligned with your values, you tap into the "fire within." The highest achievements of people and organizations arise when people feel inspired to accomplish something that fits their top values.

—Anne Greenblatt, Stanford University

"We're Not in Kansas Any More"

Nearly every employee who's been restructured, reengineered or reorganized can relate to Dorothy in *The Wizard of Oz*. Events way beyond their control, much like the cyclone, have whirled them around and deposited them in a strange land. The employee thinks, "I'm not in control. I'm not where I was. I didn't ask to be in this place. I hope I like it."

In any change, human nature and the need to pay the rent generally force us to try to adapt as quickly as possible. The problem comes about 120 days later as some employees begin to realize that adapting and adjusting and being flexible is costing them something very dear. And it will almost always be a values-related problem.

"Employees have always looked for personal satisfaction, but what may have changed in this decade is what personal satisfaction means to everyone," according to Les Taylor, program manager for Applied Materials, Inc., the human resource development institute based in Santa Clara, California. "People have really taken us back to the drawing board to revisit the top priorities in our lives. The challenge for a corporate culture, when people are visiting their values closely . . . is to be able to flex itself and create opportunities for flexibility within the company's demands."[1]

Alas

We were once conducting a career development workshop at the corporate HQ of a large, multinational bank. The participants were women and men considered to be the future leadership of the bank—all labeled as high potential—and the bank was investing heavily in their future. We were assessing values, and used an instrument called "Invest in Your Values"[2] in which each participant chose seven values from a field of 35 and applied colored stickers to them. The stickers indicated whether the value was being delivered (green sticker), was not being delivered but

(continued)

could be negotiated for or made to happen (yellow sticker), or was not possible in the future—no matter what! Those got a red sticker. As we walked around the room observing the choices people made and noticing the colored stickers, we were happy to see mostly green stickers. This indicated high satisfaction in the values delivery department. A few yellows—okay, they can be fixed, and for these high potentials, heaven itself would be moved to fix it.

But there was one red sticker on the board in front of an angry-looking young man. He pounded the red sticker down as though he was punishing the offending value itself. This young man had been pointed out to us as a shining star and an important "acquisition." He was hired particularly for his creativity, innovation and out-of-the-box thinking. And he was the only person in a room of more than 30 people who had a red sticker on one of his highest-rated values. The offending sticker was slapped onto the value word "creativity." He had indicated this to be an extremely important value. When we asked him why he put the red sticker on creativity, he said (with great vehemence and emphasis), "Because you can't be creative in this bank!"

The very reason he was hired was the reason they would lose him—they were denying him what they valued in him. If his manager had been willing to have a conversation about values with this high-potential employee, he might have been able to figure out just what the creativity-stifling problem was.

If the manager were particularly brave, another response to the creativity perception could be, "Am I stopping you?" It takes guts, but that one question, if handled well, could prevent that high-potential employee from leaving.

How can you determine which values have retention power for your employees? You can provide them with a self-paced values analysis instrument like the one used in the *Alas* story or invent your own. You can make it part of your next staff meeting or ask them any of these questions to stimulate a conversation:

TO DO . . .

Identify Employees' Values. Choose all that apply.

✓ When you go to work, what do you look forward to the most?
    a. Having new challenges
    b. Enjoying the company of my coworkers
    c. Planning my own day
    d. A relaxed, routine day

✓ When you have a new project to work on, you're excited if
    a. You will learn new things
    b. You will get to work with new people
    c. You will be in control
    d. It will be easy and low stress

✓ If you won the lottery, one thing that might keep you from quitting your job would be
    a. The excitement of competition
    b. Missing friends at work
    c. Having work goals to motivate you
    d. Not knowing what to do with your time

✓ In your ideal job, you would
    a. Have opportunities to be creative
    b. Help society
    c. Start your own business
    d. Never work more than eight hours a day

✓ Looking back, you felt most satisfied with work when
    a. You were involved in exciting projects
    b. You were helping others
    c. You worked totally independently
    d. You never had to take work home

✓ You work best when
   a. Your curiosity and energy are high
   b. You're working with a team
   c. You're working primarily alone
   d. There are no deadlines

✓ Success, to you, means
   a. Always pursuing excellence
   b. Working closely with friends
   c. Being the master of your own future
   d. Being content with your work

"**A**" answers suggest that these people are goal-oriented. Help them find opportunities to work on stimulating projects that lead to clear-cut results and a sense of accomplishment.

"**B**" answers suggest that these employees are people-oriented. Look for ways to increase their interpersonal contacts at work, perhaps through participation on task forces and project teams.

"**C**" answers indicate self-starters. Find situations that reward self-motivation with even more freedom and independence. Don't micro-manage these people.

"**D**" answers suggest that these people seek balance and an orderly work routine. Good soldiers, these people will need the greatest attention and reassurance during change.

Valuing Differences

We have looked at hundreds of transcripts from exit interviews. We were amazed at how many talented employees left because their values conflicted with those of their immediate supervisor or manager.

Sometimes as managers we tend to project our values onto our employees. But in fact it's a diversity of values that will build strength in your team. Those who value creativity will be your innovators. Those who value independence will work productively for long stretches without prodding from you. Those who value order and routine will be your dependable, solid citizens. Don't try to make the solid citizen into a creative innovator. Recognize what each person values and mine it for the sake of the whole team.

TO DO . . .

✓ Find out what matters most to your people. What do they want from their work? Ask and then listen to understand.

✓ Get creative. Customize and shift the work to better match your employees' job tasks with their values.

see UNDERSTAND

Federal Express says that listing "people" first in its corporate philosophy, *"People. Service. Profits."* is not an accident. Placing people first makes good business sense because everything is based on your ability to involve your people.[3] Retention is part art and part science. The science is knowing what to do, but the art is knowing *how* to do it.

BOTTOM LINE

Although many managers believe that money is the primary way to keep good people, it isn't. The match between your employees' values and the organization's values is a more powerful factor by far. How satisfied are your talented people with their everyday tasks? Do you know enough about your employees' values to answer that question? Values are not difficult to uncover, but they are powerful forces in an employee's decision to stay or leave. Imagine your employees as your customers. Now: What do they value most? How can you help them attain it?

Chapter 23

WELLNESS

Sustain It

To be successful there meant giving up my health and my fun and I was not willing to do that.

—A.J.

Does your organization insist on yearly physicals? Does it invest in gymnasiums, swimming pools or stress management workshops? If you're laughing, keep reading. Companies that take wellness seriously by devoting time, resources and attention find that the payoff is great, not only in retention, but in energy for the job and in productivity as well. But this chapter is not about what the corporation can do. We are interested in how you, the manager, can place your team's wellness on your own agenda.

We're not kidding ourselves. We know that by virtue of simply doing business in today's fiercely competitive environment, like it or not, we contribute to the stress that complicates our lives. But rather than

searching for a place to lay the blame, we choose to be part of the
solution that makes it possible for these two very demanding worlds
to coexist.

—Richards P. Kearns, vice chairman, Price Waterhouse LLP

Wellness and Survival of the Fittest

Today's workplace is typically a high-energy and high-productivity environment. To play successfully within it, you and your employees must be *well and fit*, mentally, emotionally and physically. In this competitive environment, wellness is a "must have" rather than a "nice to have." Without it you simply will not win. By focusing on your employees' wellness, you can increase the odds that they will stay and play effectively on your team.

What Is Wellness?

To one person, wellness means that he can enter the Boston marathon and finish in four hours. To another it may mean finally being free of migraine headaches. To another it may mean slimming down or reducing stress and high blood pressure before the next physical exam. Definitions vary.

We define wellness as a *state of physical, mental and emotional fitness*. To capture a clear picture of it, you might need to think back to a recent vacation where you felt incredibly relaxed, physically healthy and energetic, mentally sharp (maybe even creative) and emotionally satisfied. It may seem unreasonable to expect that you or your employees will feel at work like you feel on vacation, but it is useful to have the "perfect world" scenario in mind as you strive to increase your employees' fitness and wellness levels.

Wellness Manager

Show interest in your employees' well-being. Show them you care. This story illustrates what we are talking about.

see UNDERSTAND

Alas (almost)

Yolanda had recently missed several days of work and seemed uncharacteristically quiet and distant at her job. She was typically vivacious and fun-loving, and she often cheered up other team members with sagging spirits. Yolanda was still getting her work done, so her manager resisted saying anything to her about her absences or the shifts in her mood. Besides, he was concerned that to question her might somehow be crossing a line from the work world to the private world and that seemed risky to him. So he said nothing.

Three months later Yolanda tearfully handed her manager her resignation. He was shocked and told her that he did not want her to go, that she was highly valued by him and by the entire team. She seemed surprised by his response and said so. "I thought you did not care about me at all, since you never asked why I was missing work or why I seemed so sad when I did show up. I assumed that the team would be better off without me."

Yolanda's boss finally did what she had wanted him to do weeks earlier. He asked her how he could help her with whatever she was dealing with. He did not pry, but just offered to help. Yolanda began to cry (this time with gratitude) and explained that she was having health problems, and that her responsibilities as a mother and a member of his team were just more than she could handle. She said that it was truly the stress of balancing everything that was getting her down, not the illness itself.

Within minutes the resignation of a talented employee turned into a plan for how Yolanda would manage her work and family responsibilities while she regained her health. The plan included working from home two days a week, beginning work earlier in the morning, and going home early in the afternoon to take a nap. Yolanda's loyalty and commitment to her boss and her team skyrocketed, her productivity remained high, and within a few months she was back on her original schedule and feeling great.

Yolanda's boss did the right thing in the nick of time for Yolanda, the team and for himself. He dealt with the issue head on, asked what he could do and then creatively brainstormed solutions with his valuable employee. You can bet that Yolanda will not be easily enticed away to a new team or opportunity. The only thing he could have done better would have been to start sooner.

It hardly matters what the wellness challenge is for your employees. Whether it is a physical problem, an issue of stress or an emotional challenge they face, your response as a manager is the same. Ask how you can help and then collaborate to create a plan.

TO DO . . .

✓ Notice if something is wrong or if your employees' work habits change dramatically. Do not wait. Ask if there is anything you can do to help. How simple it seems and how few managers do this.

One of my most talented engineers was having major temper flare-ups and causing a lot of turmoil on the team. My boss suggested I fire him. I decided that this employee was important enough to invest in. We talked and I referred him to the Employee Assistance Program, where he got the help he needed. He has dealt with whatever was bothering him and is a joy to work with again. My supporting him through this proved to be an important statement to him and also to the team. We are stronger and more productive than ever.

—Engineering manager

✓ When an employee does tell you what is wrong, get creative and partner with that person to brainstorm solutions and create a plan to remedy the situation.

I hire knowledge workers (people who work with their brains). If they are unhappy or not feeling well, they show up with half a brain—

I cannot afford that. I work very hard to keep my employees happy and healthy!

—CEO of a California software company

The "B" Word

Balance between one's work and personal life continues to be a recognized contributor to wellness and one of the most challenging topics for the wellness-minded manager to tackle. One team we know about has spent so much time in recent years dealing with the issue of balance that they now call it the "B" word. It is almost off-limits as a discussion topic because it seems there are few solutions and they became "sick of talking about it."

We believe, though, that you *need to talk about it*—and think about it—and even do something about it! What does balance mean to you and to your employees? (It is different for everyone.)

Alan Quarry, president of Quarry Communications in Waterloo, Canada, has a way of "doing something about it." He gives each of the 90 members of his team $150.00 a year to do something (anything!) to bring balance into their lives. His only request: tell me how you've used the money. The ways in which employees spend the money underscore how individual our balance needs are. Employees report spending their money on ballroom dance lessons, a drum set, gardening tools, instruction in tai-chi and kick-boxing. All in all, it is not a lot for him to spend, and the message he sends is crystal clear. Do you have a discretionary budget that might be spent this way?

We are not suggesting that your employees' balance issues are your concern alone, or that you must provide the answers. We *are* suggesting, however, that there are actions you can take to encourage balance and thus wellness.

*Imagine life as a game in which you are juggling five balls in the air. You name them—*work, family, health, friends *and* spirit—*you're* *keeping all of these in the air. You will soon understand that work is a rubber ball. If you drop it, it will bounce back. But the other four balls, family, health, friends and spirit, are made of glass. If you drop one of these, it will be irrevocably scuffed, marked, nicked, damaged or even shattered. It will never be the same. You must understand that.*

—Brian Dyson, CEO of Coca-Cola Enterprises

Overwhelm Is an Understatement

The pressures to do more with less, to move faster than the competition, to be more creative, more innovative, more distinct, to do it with fewer dollars, and to be available at all times, push many to say that work just asks too much.

Alas

A senior manager in a healthcare organization noticed that he was snapping at his employees, having trouble sleeping and feeling generally not up to speed. When a friend asked him how he was spending his time away from work, he answered, "What time away from work?" In the past he had spent evenings at home and enjoyed movies, friends, books and music to relax. He had worked out at the gym four nights a week. All of that seemed a distant memory now. His new boss had set the tone: We work late every night (for those who are even remotely ambitious or committed to the organization). So much for balance and wellness. The results for this senior manager included his employees being fed up with his grumpiness (two had recently quit), lower productivity than ever (maybe because he was exhausted), constant headaches and increasing resentment toward his boss and the organization. Recently he has begun to check out the Internet job postings, thinking that there must be a saner place to work!

This senior manager will be gone soon, having found a workplace where balance is at least a topic of discussion and where his boss expects that people have a life outside of work.

So what about you? What example do you set as a manager and what do you expect from your people? Ask yourself these questions:

✓ Do I uphold a value system that promotes workaholism? Am I a workaholic?
✓ Do I expect my employees to travel or work on weekends? How often?
✓ Do I hold numerous early morning or early evening meetings?
✓ Do I compliment employees for their long hours or, instead, for the quality work they complete?

How did you do? Often managers discourage balance by the examples they set or by what they expect and reward. Just take note of your own behaviors and ask if you are encouraging or discouraging balance for your employees.

TO DO . . .

✓ *Set the example you want them to follow.* Be conscious of your own behaviors and the expectations those behaviors set for your employees. If you want them to have more balance in their lives, you have to model it. Share what you do to achieve balance in your life. Your employees may think that you have none. (We hope they're wrong.)
✓ *Hold a balance discussion* at your next staff meeting (or in one-on-one meetings.) Dedicate the whole meeting to the topic.
✓ *Ask people what they juggle* in their lives and what matters most to them. (Be ready to hear that work is *not the number one priority* for many of them.)
✓ *Support your employees in achieving balance.* Encourage the activities that they love; ask about their golf lessons or their children's school plays.

Stretched and Stressed

Hans Selye, the founder of the field of stress management, said, "To be free of stress is to be dead." We agree that just *living* is often stressful. But Selye and other leaders in the stress management field have found that although optimum levels of stress produce peak performance, overdoses can definitely lead to poor performance and even to illness.

In organizations we seldom see a problem of too little stress. We sometimes see the optimum stress level and high performance results. Most often, however, we see stress overload and negative results, on health and on productivity. There seems to be a high correlation between lack of balance and stress. Where balance is missing, the workload typically appears to be very high and stressful. When people have balanced lives, they seem to have less work stress or they just manage it better. So what can you as a manager do to reduce stress for your employees?

TO DO . . .

✓ Be aware and watchful for signs of excess stress. When you think you see it in your employees, ask them how they are doing (or feeling). They will appreciate your asking the question and may confide in you.

> *He seemed so uptight and distracted. I called him in to my office and asked if there was anything I could do. He confided in me. Well, actually, he just started venting! I listened and empathized as he poured out his frustration, anger and disappointment. An hour later, he thanked me, said he felt 100 percent better and headed back to work. I guess he just needed me to listen and quietly support him.*
>
> —Manager, manufacturing Company

✓ Once you know what's going on, you can partner with the employee to solve the problem. Be open and willing to think outside the box as you search for ways to relieve stress. Brainstorm possible solutions *with* your employees. Consider some of these stress management options with them:

- Shift some of the work to others if possible. Think about who could help and how to ask for the help.
- Take more breaks. Get up, move around, go for a quick walk.
- Learn relaxation, visualization and/or breathing techniques. Take a stress management class or yoga.
- Exercise as a way to relieve stress. Join a gym or take up power walking or jogging.
- Seek professional help and/or counseling.
- Get enough sleep, eat well and reduce stress-producing chemicals like caffeine and nicotine.
- Take a vacation.

✓ Support your employees as they implement some stress management techniques. For example, if Mike decides he needs to take two 15-minute brisk walks during the day to relieve stress, be sure that you reward his actually doing it. Your support will pay off.

✓ Take a stand to reduce stress.

One of my colleagues was an abusive boss and he had recently lost two key workers. I saw the stress level continue to rise on his team, and I finally decided to speak up about it. He calmed down considerably (with some prompting by his boss) and the stress level diminished greatly. I felt a little weird about intervening the way I had, but his employees were so grateful—and we did not lose any more of them!

—Accounting manager

BOTTOM LINE

If your employees are well, you are far more likely to have a well-functioning organization. Your best employees will work hard, produce for you *and stick around* in an environment that promotes their health and fitness—emotional, mental and physical.

Chapter 24

X-ERS

Handle with Care

I saw three young talented employees pack their bags and leave, mostly because we were just too rigid and tended to micromanage them. We should have loosened up a bit.

—A.J.

Warning! This chapter contains generalizations, even stereotyping. We know that you know that the needs of X-ers in most ways reflect the needs of all workers. Yet we believe this demographic group does have some unique features worth talking and thinking about.

If you're not one of them, they can seem at times to be another species. Generation X challenges some managers with values and work habits that are often baffling. You may wonder what they really want or need and how you can possibly deliver it. Yet we know that this generation has most of the same hopes and ambitions of prior generations. They are the same, and yet different somehow.

The expectations of all workers appear to be shifting, and X-ers have been a major catalyst of the change. They have set the tone for emerging workers of all ages. A key question regarding X-er employees is,

"How can you maximize their potential and encourage them to stay on your team?" That question certainly applies to all of your employees, but some of the answers for X-ers may seem new to you.

The Making of an X-er

In order to understand them, it is valuable to understand what they grew up with. If you're a senior worker, you have watched the tremendous pace of change over the last 30 years shape the world of work. During the last half of the 1960s, space exploration and its technological applications affected work life. The social consciousness of the 1970s shifted during the 1980s to a focus on the acquisition of money. Within the context of the organization, the social contract between employer and employee dissolved. During these significant shifts approximately 44.5 million Americans were born (between 1965 and 1976) and grew up. They were labeled Generation X in a novel written by Vancouver, B.C. author Douglas Copeland.

Generation X experienced a childhood fraught with uncertainty. Many were latchkey kids, who from a very young age were responsible for themselves after school. Many grew up in single-parent households. Raised on video games, TV, MTV, and computers, they learned to digest information coming at them rapidly from many sources. Having witnessed corporate downsizing, the demise of lifetime employment, and the price of neglecting family in favor of work, many in this new generation have declared, "Not me!" They reflect a shift, conscious or not, from unyielding loyalty and commitment toward the organization to loyalty to oneself. For them, commitment to the organization is based upon mutuality.

The result of the changes within the last 30 years is a new mind-set toward work and what is now defined as a career. Senior workers lived these changes first-hand and felt their abruptness. X-ers have been watching, learning and adapting to what their parents experienced.

During X-ers' lifetime, finding and retaining educated and skilled employees has become a tremendous challenge. People have become the most important asset in the organization. They provide the competitive edge. Yet many organizations have held onto the old model, demanding loyalty but offering no guarantees. Generation X employees have read between the lines. They believe it is now up to the organization, to you the manager, to understand them, leverage their potential *and retain them!*

Here are some keys to how X-ers think, but remember: Many X-er characteristics also hold true for workers of any age.

Multiple Jobs Make a Career

When older workers look at an X-er's resume they often conclude, "A job-hopper," or "No loyalty there." The work history may look fragmented to an older hiring manager but makes perfect sense to the X-er. The now-outdated wisdom about resumes was that they should reflect longevity within a given organization. For X-ers, the organization is a place to learn new skills and build experience, a springboard to a new opportunity there or elsewhere. Many X-ers' resumes reflect this reality, showing five or six jobs within the same span of years.

> *I'll stay here as long as I learn new skills and feel like I am a part of this organization. I have thought about leaving many times before, but the one thing that holds me here is that I am constantly challenged on an intellectual basis. I see this position and the skills I have gained from this position as just one piece of the puzzle that is my entire career. I have absolutely no misgivings about the fact that this organization is not my final resting place. In fact I couldn't imagine being tied down to just one company over my career lifetime.*
>
> —Tanya, 28-year-old project manager

Money Talks—Or Does It?

Monetary compensation is *very* important. However, salary does not stand alone as an incentive. It will take more than just greenbacks to lure and hold on to your Gen-X employee. Most X-ers want to know:

1. What new skills can be learned? How will this job build my resume?
2. Does the job fit within the context of my larger career goals?
3. Does the position fit with my personal interests and values?
4. Will the position offer me ongoing challenges and the opportunity to contribute and be recognized within the organization?
5. What's the pay?

see VALUES

> *Rick, a 28-year-old freelance graphic artist, recently turned down a lucrative opportunity. "I was offered a contract to do all the graphic work for a quickly growing software company in northern California. I declined the job because it called for an artistic style that I had been using for years at my previous job. I started my own business because I wanted to pursue work that reflected my own style. I could have easily agreed to the new contract. However, it would have felt like I was selling out. Obviously, it is important to me to offer my clients what they want, but it is equally important to feel like I am doing what is right for me.*

Freedom and Feedback Are Part of the Deal

Gen-X-ers want to have a clear understanding of the expectations for a position or project. At the same time, once expectations are established and deliverables are defined, *they need to have space, resources and the freedom to produce the desired results.* This is not a demand to "do it my way or I'll hit the highway." Rather, X-ers are focused on how to learn and succeed. Perhaps this is why X-ers prefer ongoing feedback rather than occasional formal reviews. As a logical extension of their other preferences, most X-ers do not tolerate micromanagement. (Many of you are saying, "This is all true for workers at any age." You're right. But it is absolutely critical to remember if you want to keep your talented X-ers.)

Mom: *(calling 27-year-old son at work)* Is it okay if I call you at work?
Son: *(silence, as if trying to understand the question)*
Mom: I mean, are you allowed to take personal calls?
Son: I'd better be.

He was truly mystified by the question. It was unthinkable to be constrained by such a weird rule. These seemingly small things could make the difference between staying and leaving for an X-er. A senior employee may not like the rule, but he would probably complain quietly and stay despite it.

Loyalty Is Out, Mutuality Is In

X-ers witnessed the demise of the concept of lifetime employment. Many saw their loyal, dedicated parents get laid off during massive downsizing. They recognize that today's organizational reality calls for independence and self-reliance. X-ers know that most organizations wouldn't think twice about letting someone go who was not living up to potential. By the same token, many X-ers wouldn't think twice about leaving an organization that wasn't *allowing them* to live up to their potential.

Alas

The pay was good. The location was great. But I knew I could do much more. They wanted me to keep doing what I was doing. So I left.

—X-er in high-tech company

The X-er does not subscribe to traditional loyalty. What the X-er does offer is a sense of loyalty through mutuality. They often have dedication and a willingness to do what the job requires, but within the context of partnership. You can initiate this "new loyalty" by creating relationships that build upon individual interests and shared goals.

Show and Tell, Tell, Tell

Once the property of bosses and those "who need to know," information has become a commodity that X-ers expect. Raised in an environment of constant stimulus from multiple sources, X-ers are conditioned to getting the information they want and need. Withholding information that an X-er feels is relevant to a project damages trust and incentive. Conversely, sharing relevant information and filling in the gaps builds trust, encourages creativity and motivates the X-er to take ownership of a project's results.

Work and Play—Both Belong at Work

I want a fat salary, a signing bonus, and a cappuccino machine. Oh, and I'm bringing my bird to work. I'm the New Organization Man. You need me.
> —Roberto Ziche, cover of *Fortune*, March 16, 1998

see KICKS

To X-ers, work does not necessarily exclude play. They want to be part of a work environment that inspires fun and creativity. X-ers take balance very seriously in their work and personal lives. Although some people have labeled this generation "slackers" who are not willing to pay their dues, X-ers can be the first to roll up their sleeves and work until the sun comes up. They view work as a cycle in which there are times to give your all and times to kick back. They watched their parents work full speed ahead, and for what?

So if you manage X-ers, how can you keep them on board?

TO DO . . .

✓ **X**-tend yourself. Ask their opinions and really listen to what they have to say. Xers may be the first ones to jump ship if they feel they're not being heard.

✓ Set **X**-pectations. Make sure the rules of the game are clear. Define which elements of a job are fixed and which are flexible. Establish guidelines and then step to the sidelines.

✓ **X**-plain not just "how" but "why." Establish how a specific job is to be done, but give X-ers an understanding of the larger picture. Providing a context for how a specific task or project fits within the entire organization creates greater ownership and understanding of a job's value.

✓ **X**-press yourself. Provide ongoing feedback. Traditional performance reviews don't work for the X-er. Make it casual and informal, yet with a clear purpose and outcome. Weekly project reviews make more sense and are more relevant to X-ers' immediate needs.

✓ **X**-pand the possibilities. Provide challenge and opportunities that give them a sense of responsibility and recognition. To X-ers, prolonged tedious assignments wear thin. Allocate specific problem-solving tasks or ask X-ers to create a plan or new idea.

Use these strategies with *all* of your employees. And use "A–Z" strategies from this book with your X-ers.

Note from the Authors

Tara Mello served as a key resource for this book. She did research and editing and was a critical sounding board and catalyst throughout the writing process. She is an X-er. We asked her why she stayed with us for months, even though the pay was low. Here is her response:

> *I remain on this project because it stretches my creativity. When we get together, even over the phone, and begin to talk about the concepts behind the book and how they all fit together, I get energized. What I am learning is not what you would traditionally learn from a mentor or manager. Instead, I get the experience of two very successful self-employed women. From that I get ideas about how to make my business more successful as well as how to balance work and family life.*

My interest in the topic is also a reason why I stay. I have learned tons about retention and its related topics, so much so that I am confident I'd have a high retention rate with my employees if I were a manager. I already used strategies in this book to help retain the adult volunteers for the Cub Scout Pack I help oversee.

The last reason has to do with meaningful work and making a difference. I see so much tension and frustration from people in the corporate world today and I know it's not healthy. (It certainly wasn't for me.) If this project helps others who choose the corporate route to find a better fit, then I will feel that my work has been worth all the effort.

BOTTOM LINE

The challenge of retaining Gen-X employees will continue. While their wants may not differ from those of other employees, X-ers are more willing to say what they want and to leave if you don't deliver. They're the first generation to reject organizational loyalty outright. In its place, the opportunity for something richer and far more rewarding has emerged: collaborative relationships between employer and employee based upon shared goals. We can thank Generation X for bringing this gift to the workplace.

Chapter 25

Yield

Power Down

Too bad my boss always needed to be right!

—A.J.

Think about the highway on-ramps in a busy city, or an intersection with no stop signs, or a line forming at the movies. When someone says, "No, you go first," with a smile and gesture, we think how remarkable and rare that action is.

Similarly, in many workplaces, yielding is all too rare. It appears that most managers want to hang on to their power, prestige, importance or decision-making authority once they finally have it. In the short term it may feel great to be so important or powerful, but there will be costs in the long term.

Research and our own experience teach us that when you yield occasionally to your employees, you empower them to think for themselves, to be more creative, more enthusiastic and probably more productive. Your employees' enthusiasm and sense of value as team members will increase the odds that they will stick around.

Power Down? I Just Got Powered Up!

A sense of newly found power is one of the joys of being promoted into a leadership role where you manage one or hundreds of employees. Even if you were never consciously looking to be more powerful, it may be ego-gratifying to be anointed as one who is deemed skilled enough to make bigger decisions, direct others' activities and even take the spotlight bows for team successes.

Once you receive that kind of power, it might be difficult to give some away. Many of our role models taught us to hang on to that power—to wield it fairly (the benevolent dictator type)—but never to give it away. Then management books in the 1980s proclaimed *empowerment*, and with it came confusion for many managers, who asked, "Why should I let my employees make more decisions, take more credit, be in charge? And once you tell me why, tell me *how* to empower my people."

So let's take a look at these two critical questions: Why yield and how can you yield?

Why Yield? What's In It for You?

This case study highlights several benefits of yielding.

Alas

A manager in a leading drug research and development company (we'll call her Joan) woke up one morning and recognized that 20 percent of her employees were doing 80 percent of the thinking. She was concerned for a number of reasons:

✔ *The 80 percent of her employees who weren't really using their creative and intellectual abilities also seemed to be somewhat apathetic,*

(continued)

disengaged or just going through the motions at work. Their job satisfaction level seemed low, and in many cases she knew they could be more productive if they were more involved somehow in the work.

✓ *The competition would gain an edge if her company didn't utilize talent better, get more creative and stay on the cutting edge.*

✓ *She and a handful of thinking employees were overstretched and spent much of their time answering questions and meeting with others to solve their problems.*

✓ *She had lost some talented employees and learned in the exit interviews that they were not being challenged enough and had grown bored.*

What is wrong with this picture?

Joan knew:

✓ She needed to leverage the brilliance and creativity in her group.

✓ She needed to reduce apathy and get people more engaged in their work.

✓ She needed to increase job satisfaction and all the benefits connected to it (like productivity).

✓ She needed to free up her time—and that of some of her other *thinking* employees—spent answering questions and making decisions for others.

✓ She needed to retain her talent!

With some assessment of her situation, Joan knew she had to do something to meet these goals. It took her a while to realize that her solution was right in front of her all the time. We'll look at what Joan did to solve her problem in a minute. For now, look at your situation.

TO DO . . .

Check out this list:

✓ Is your organization lean and mean, like so many others after a decade of downsizing?

✓ Is your span of control larger than ever and are the expectations from above constantly increasing your workload and pressure?

✓ Do some of your employees seem apathetic or less than eager to show up on Monday mornings?

✓ Are many of your employees still waiting to be told what to do every step of the way?

✓ Have you lost any of your talented team members because they were bored or needed a new challenge?

✓ Is the competition nipping at your heels?

see OPPORTUNITIES

If your answers are no, then either you are already yielding power to your employees or you aren't yet feeling the pressure to do so. If that's the case, move on to another chapter to focus on something that matters more right now or that you may not already be doing quite as well.

If you answered yes to four or more on the checklist, then read on. You have just identified the reasons to power down. You must yield to and empower your people in order to compete successfully. And you must yield in order to keep your talented employees on your team.

In an empowered organization it will be the manager's job to coach and guide the people in how to do a task and get them the resources. The manager will work for his/her subordinates.
—Alan Greenberg, American Management Association

Who's Got the Right of Way?

You may be convinced that you could benefit by giving more power to your employees yet find it difficult to know where to start. The rules can be fuzzy or hard to remember, just like the road rules that guide merging onto a busy highway or crossing an intersection that has no stop signs.

In the matter of powering down to your employees, the uncertainty is even greater because there *are no rules*. Your organization establishes cultural norms and role models, but as an individual manager you have tremendous leeway to give power.

Let's take another look at the case study to see how Joan yielded.

Alas Revisited

Joan realized that she needed to get at least 80 percent of her people doing the thinking, not 20 percent. She analyzed why they waited for direction, came to her for answers and basically let their brains take extended breaks day after day. One conclusion was shocking: she was a big part of the problem!

Joan had been promoted because she was bright and a good leader. It was incredibly gratifying to be given a much larger span of control, more people to manage, a large budget and her own office. She had an open door policy and encouraged her people to come to her anytime with their problems and questions. Joan felt important and brilliant as she repeatedly solved day-to-day problems that her employees brought her. (Ever felt like that?) It dawned on her that she had been rewarding their "sleepy brain syndrome." Why should they think if she would do it for them?

So Joan did just one thing to power down. She hung a sign on her door that looked like this:

What? That's it? End of story? Well, yes, basically. Joan explained to her employees that she had been underserving and undervaluing them by answering all of their questions and giving them step-by-step direction. She admitted to them that she had also robbed the organization of tremendous intellectual and creative capital by giving answers instead of asking questions. So when people came through her open door and asked their questions as they always had, she pointed to the sign and asked them powerful, thought-provoking questions. Questions like:

What do you think the problem is?

Who do you think should be involved in solving this issue?

What are the choices we have?

These questions empowered people to solve problems creatively, to lean on each other instead of on the boss and to come up with multiple options and possibilities. She gave encouragement and praise as people struggled to produce outstanding, creative solutions and innovative new approaches. Her team's productivity and retention rates surpassed all others in the organization. Other managers came to her to find out what she was doing to magically inspire such phenomenal results.

Joan chuckled as she related the secret of her success. "I had to set aside my ego. I could not be the all-knowing sage if I wanted my employees' brains to keep functioning. I truly had to yield to them, to accept them as brilliant, eager-to-succeed colleagues. I had to power down, give them some of my previously guarded power and importance. The result is that we all win. My job is easier and more gratifying and our results are the best ever. The best part is my most talented people are happier and more motivated than ever before and they plan to stick around as long as the fun continues."

There is more to Joan's approach than meets the eye. The "No Answers" sign could be an annoyance if the follow-through did not include key elements:

1. Trust your employees to come up with the answers. Even if you would have done it another way, consider the approaches they create and support them all the way.

2. Manage your reactions when you yield and they crash! Powering down and yielding are sometimes risky and there *will* be failures. Instead of punishing, collaborate with your empowered employee to learn from the mistake or failure. Focus on what could be done differently next time around, rather than the rearview mirror approach of what should have been done.

    A senior manager made a mistake that cost his company 10 million dollars. As he walked into his boss's office he anticipated anger and most probably a firing. His boss asked him what he had learned from the mistake, and he quickly listed all the things he would do differently next time. Then he waited for the ax to fall. And he waited. Finally he asked, "Aren't you going to fire me?" The boss answered, "Why would I fire you? I just invested 10 million dollars in your learning."

3. Serve your employees. Be available and be a resource to them. To yield doesn't mean you take the next exit. Empowerment spells disaster in too many cases where the manager tosses decisions and workloads at his employees and then moves on to bigger things. The "No Answers" approach works only if you are willing to work with your employees, to brainstorm with them when they are stumped, and to give them guidance and feedback along the way.

4. See them as colleagues more often than as subordinates. Show it by occasionally doing work that may seem "beneath you."

    A Southwest Airlines pilot was chatting with a young couple with a baby in the front seat of the airplane. The luggage was being loaded when the young mother realized that the baby's bottle was in the checked luggage, not the carry-on bag. She looked frantically out the window and spotted the blue suitcase. The pilot asked which one was theirs and then scrambled down the stairs onto the tarmac to retrieve the bottle. The young woman and the pilot exchanged signals while he found the suitcase, opened it and found the bottle. As he entered the plane with the prize, the flight attendants and passengers who had been watching burst into applause. He could have asked a flight attendant to do it, but think what he gained by yielding, by powering down and just doing it himself.

5. Give the spotlight away. (No, we're not contradicting ourselves. We're just giving you another option.) This may be the toughest of all. As the hero, you may have received the applause from your employees and they may have credited you with the team's success. Powering down means sharing the stage *and the applause* with your team members. Ironically, your stock will go up with your employees as you increasingly give them room to perform (and get credit for) brilliant, creative work.

Nordstrom managers yield by letting employees practice what the employee handbook preaches: "Use your own best judgment at all times." A manager told the story of her employee returning late from a lunch break, out of breath. When asked why she was out of breath (not why she was late) the employee responded, "One of my pregnant customers ordered a new bathrobe and it just came in. When I called to tell her about it, I found out she went to the hospital this morning to give birth, so I decided to use my lunch break and run it over to her." The customer wrote an appreciation letter to Nordstrom's senior management, and the employee, in turn, was recognized and rewarded for her outstanding customer service.

Do you ever see that kind of customer service in a tightly controlled, micromanaged environment? Probably not. And count on it: empowered employees will have great ideas or take on tasks you may not have asked them to perform. They will put their own signatures on excellence. They may even take your breath away.

BOTTOM LINE

Yielding will increase the odds of retaining your best people. As folks are given more power to create, make decisions and truly affect the success of the team, their job satisfaction (and your odds of keeping them) will go up. At the same time, your ability to compete successfully and accomplish your business goals will increase. You have phenomenal power to yield. Try it and see what happens.

Chapter 26

ZENITH

Go For It

One of my best employees gave notice yesterday. And I thought I knew all there was to know about retaining key people! I'm determined to create a place where this is not the norm.

—A.J.

You've done it. You're at Z. You may have come here through any number of routes. Some of you diligently read each of the chapters in this book. Others have skimmed, scanned, and landed here. Others came immediately to Z because they like to read the last first.

Whichever path brought you here, we have a series of questions for you to answer. For those who have read all the chapters, or even skimmed them, these questions will show you how much you've absorbed, and what work you may still need to do. For those who start here, this inventory will direct you to the specific chapters you may want to read first. In any case, this self-test is for you.

Each question addresses the main theme of that chapter (A to Z). We ask you to be honest and to ask yourself if you (still?) hold these beliefs about managing others. Each question is designed to capture the essence of the retention philosophy and strategies outlined in that particular chapter. (Note: It is impossible to end up with a *no* for all of the 26 questions.)

What's Your RPI?

Retention Probability Index: A Manager's Self-Test

If you checked yes, read:	Do you...		
	Yes	No	
ASK	A. ☐	☐	Feel that you shouldn't "ask" unless you're sure you can do something with the answer?
BUCK	B. ☐	☐	Believe that keeping good people is out of your hands?
CAREERS	C. ☐	☐	Agree that although coaching should be continual, your people are adults and they should know where they need to improve?
DIGNITY	D. ☐	☐	Wonder how you are supposed to recognize so many different individual needs?
ENRICH	E. ☐	☐	Believe that it's really difficult to enrich most jobs?
FAMILY	F. ☐	☐	Agree that most employees don't want to mix family and personal life with work life?
GOALS	G. ☐	☐	Believe that most employees only want to move up?
HIRE	H. ☐	☐	Think that a skill match when hiring is the most essential match to be made?
INFORMATION	I. ☐	☐	Believe that there's a good deal of big picture information that is best not shared with employees?
JERK	J. ☐	☐	Think that employees aren't really that sensitive to what you say or do?
KICKS	K. ☐	☐	Tend not to join in the fun when others are taking breaks, sharing jokes, relaxing from the stress of it all?
LINK	L. ☐	☐	Fear that connecting your people with folks in other departments will eventually pull them away from yours?
MENTOR	M. ☐	☐	Feel that there just isn't time to tell them your story or give them your views, considering all there is to be done?
NUMBERS	N. ☐	☐	Believe that all these retention efforts aren't really worth the time you spend on them?

O.	☐	☐	Agree that opportunities for growth are limited?	OPPORTUNITIES
P.	☐	☐	Find little time to talk with your people about the degree to which they are doing what they really want to do?	PASSION
Q.	☐	☐	Believe that going "outside the box" is difficult in your organization?	QUESTION
R.	☐	☐	Believe that small recognition efforts don't help very much?	REWARD
S.	☐	☐	Feel more comfortable knowing exactly what your employees do with their time during the work day?	SPACE
T.	☐	☐	Agree that it's just more comfortable for you not to be too direct when giving feedback?	TRUTH
U.	☐	☐	Feel that you listen about as well as most, and you can't get much better at it?	UNDERSTANDING
V.	☐	☐	Think that it's crossing a personal boundary to find out more about what your people value?	VALUES
W.	☐	☐	Think that wellness is being addressed primarily by corporate gyms and stress-management programs?	WELLNESS
X.	☐	☐	Throw up your hands when trying to understand young employees?	X-ERS
Y.	☐	☐	Truly find it difficult to share power or the limelight?	YIELD
Z.	☐	☐	Think this retention stuff is another fad, and it, like others, will go away soon?	ZENITH

So, how do you score? Here is how to make sense of the test and decide what to do next.

TO DO . . .

✓ **Score the RPI.** If your *nos* outnumber your *yeses*, you're on the right track. If your *yeses* far outnumber your *nos*, you've got work to do. Highlight the *yeses* and turn to the chapters that are referenced. Read (or reread) them and look for just one or two ideas or strategies that you might try next in your own work group. Start there. Work, focus and have patience. It takes at least six weeks to develop a new habit.

I realized that in general I have created a pretty good retention culture. But as open as I thought I was, I also see that I need to work on giving people more space. Space to do the work in their own way, as long as they get the results. And even some space to flex their work hours whenever possible. That's my focus for the next few months.

—Team leader, manufacturing organization

✓ ***Get feedback.*** As you try something new it may feel strange at first. Get input from your trusted employees or colleagues. Ask them to tell you what's working and what's not.

I decided that I need to show people that I care about them and respect the work that they do for me. At first, when I wandered into their work area just to ask how things were going, they nervously looked at me, waiting for some criticism or concern to come out of my mouth. After a few weeks, though, they loosened up and warmed up. I asked for feedback and one of the more vocal employees told me that he and others have noticed the change in my behavior and they really appreciate it. That positive input keeps me going.

—Manager, engineering firm

✓ ***Reward yourself and choose again.*** Acknowledge your success. Give yourself the praise you deserve. Then choose another strategy to work on.

I've worked on mentoring, and have definitely improved. I've patted myself on the back, and my employees' reactions to me are an even greater reward. Next, I'm taking on fun. We have been all work, no play for too long. I think I'll start the ball rolling by ordering pizza this

Friday afternoon and turning off the phones. I plan to just chat with my team about how we can enjoy work more. I'm sure they'll have some great ideas.

—Owner, executive search firm

The Zenith—The Best

The idea for this chapter struck us as we were working with an organization that believed in holding what they called "zenith" meetings. Zenith meetings are typically called by senior managers. They are used to bring together three or four disparate teams or people for the purpose of working out the ideal scenario, the best strategy, or the high point around which all will have energy and commitment. At zenith meetings you don't stop until you find that point. You simply keep at it.

We hope you will keep at it. Build a workplace so productive and fulfilling that your talented people will want to stay, create, and make their mark. That's the Zenith.

We have done all we can do. Now it's up to you.

—Bev & Sharon

P. S. Write and tell us what happened at http://www.keepem.com

Notes

Chapter 1: Ask

1. Gina Imperato, "35 Ways to Land a Job Online," *Fast Company* 16 (August 1998): 140.

Chapter 2: Buck

1. Marie Gendron, "Keys to Retaining Your Best Managers in a Tight Job Market," *Harvard Management Update* (June 1998): 1–4.
2. Hay Group, "1998–1999 Employee Attitudes Study," 8, *HR/OD*, (December 1, 1998).

    "Why Workers Quit," *Arizona Republic,* 26 July 1998.

    "Money Can't Buy Employee Commitment, WFD Research Reveals," *Business Wire,* 4 August 1998.
3. "Study of the Emerging Workforce," Saratoga Institute, Interim Services, Inc., 1997.
4. "Retention Management: Strategies, Practices, Trends," American Management Association, Saratoga Institute, New York, 1997, p. 31.
5. John A. Challenger, "There Is No Future for the Workplace," *The Futurist* 32 (October 1, 1998): 16–20.

Chapter 5: Enrich

1. Dana Fields, "At Harley, Workers are Boss," *Detroit News,* 12 June 1998.
2. Beverly Kaye, *Up Is Not the Only Way* (Palo Alto, CA: Davies Black, 1997).

Chapter 6: Family

1. Elizabeth Sheley, "Flexible Work Options: Factors that Make Them Work," *HR Magazine* (February 1996).
2. Ibid.
3. Colleen Mastony, "Executive Moms," *Forbes* 162 (July 6, 1998).

Chapter 9: Information

1. Sandar Larkin and P. J. Larkin, *Communicating Change: How to Win Employee Support for New Business Directions* (New York: McGraw Hill, 1994): 14–15.
2. Loren Gary, "Enlisting Hearts and Minds," *Harvard Management Update* (February 1997).
3. Jack Stack, *Great Game of Business* (Bo Burlingham, 1994).
4. Bill Catlette and Richard Hadden, *Contented Cows Give Better Milk* (Germantown, TN: Saltillo Press, 1988), 61.
5. Sharon Wohlfarth, "Managers Need Two-Way Communication with Workers," *Kansas City Business Journal* (June 8, 1998).
6. Marshall Colt, "How Communication Can Prevent Lawsuits," *Denver Business Journal* (August 10, 1998).

Chapter 11: Kicks

1. "Study of the Emerging Workforce," Saratoga Institute, Interim Services, Inc., 1997.
2. Jackie Frieberg and Kevin Frieberg, *Nuts!* (Austin, TX: Bard Press, 1996), 247.

3. Susan Vaughn, "To Think Out of the Box, Get Back Into the Sandbox," *Los Angeles Times*, 11 January 1999, Careers section, pp. 3, 13.

Chapter 12: Link

1. Gillian Flynn, "Rhino's Owner Explains the Company's Purpose," *Personnel Journal* 75 (July 1996): 36–43.
2. Christina Melnarik, "Retaining High Tech Professionals: Constructive and Destructive Responses to Job Dissatisfaction Among Electrical Engineers and Non-Engineering Professionals" (Ph.D. diss., Walden University, 1998).
3. David Krackhardt and Jeffrey Hanson, "Informal Networks: The Company Behind the Chart," *Harvard Business Review* 71 (July/August 1993): 111.
4. Beverly Kaye and Beverly Bernstein, "Mentworking: Building Learning Relationships for the 21st Century," workshop materials, Career Systems International, Scranton, PA, 1998, 45.
5. Ibid, 67.

Chapter 13: Mentor

1. Jennifer Reingold, "Why Your Workers Might Jump Ship," *Business Week* (March 1, 1999): 6.
2. Beverly Kaye, adapted from "Career Development—Anytime, Anyplace," *Training & Development* 47 (December 1993): 46–50.

Chapter 15: Opportunities

1. Sharon Jordan-Evans and Beverly Kaye, "Opportunity Mine-ing," workshop materials, Career Systems International, Scranton, PA, 1998.
2. Edward F. Murphy, *2,715 One-Line Quotations for Speakers, Writers, and Raconteurs* (New York: Crown, 1981), 148.

3. Robert H. Waterman, Jr., Judith A. Waterman, and Betsy A. Collard, "Toward a Resilient Work Force," *Harvard Business Review* 72 (July/August 1994): 87–95.

4. Edward F. Murphy, *2,715 One-Line Quotations for Speakers, Writers, and Raconteurs* (New York: Crown, 1981).

Chapter 16: Passion

1. Jackie Frieberg and Kevin Frieberg, *Nuts!* (Austin, TX: Bard Press, 1996), 10.

Chapter 18: Reward

1. Ken Blanchard and Spencer Johnson, *The One Minute Manager* (New York: William Morrow, 1982).

Chapter 19: Space

1. Jennifer Oldham, "Remote Control," *Los Angeles Times*, 8 June 1998.

2. James C. Collins and Jerry I. Porras, *Built to Last* (New York: Harper Business, 1994), 119.

3. Harriet Johnson Brackey, "It's About Time: New Ways to Reshape the Work Week," *Miami Herald*, 1 June 1998.

Chapter 20: Truth

1. Morgan W. McCall, Michael M. Lombardo, and A. Morrison, *The Lessons of Experience* (Lexington, MA: Lexington Books, 1988).

Morgan W. McCall, *High Flyers* (Cambridge, MA: Harvard Business School Press, 1998).

2. Jerry Hirshberg, *The Creative Priority: Driving Innovative Business in the Real World* (New York: HarperCollins, 1998).

Chapter 21: Understand

1. Madelyn Burley-Allen, *Listening: The Forgotten Skill* (New York: Wiley, 1995), 14.

Chapter 22: Values

1. Katherine Thornberry, "Valley Firms Get Creative to Retain Hot Employees," *Business Journal of San Jose* (June 1, 1998).
2. "Invest in Your Values: A Self Assessment Instrument," Career Systems International, 1999.
3. D. Keith Denton, *Recruitment, Retention and Employee Relations* (Westport, CT: Quorum Books, 1992) 48.

About the Authors

The authors of this book are friends and colleagues. They are also consultants, mothers, wives, siblings and daughters. They're different (very) and similar (very). They've taught each other a lot. Sharon, for example, is Bev's role model for Balance, Balance, Balance. Bev is Sharon's role model for Build, Build, Build. They are both passionate about the message in this book and about their retention research and work.

Bev (left) now serves as president of Career Systems International, a publisher of career development tools, as well as president of Beverly Kaye and Associates Inc., a consulting and training company she started in the late 1970s. Her first book, *Up Is Not the Only Way*, became a classic in the field. It was first published in 1982, and again by Davies Black in 1997. Her consulting interests all fall under the wide banner of development. She holds a doctorate from UCLA. Beverly (originally from New Jersey) lives in Sherman Oaks, California, with her husband Barry, and preteen daughter, Lindsey.

Sharon (right) now serves as the president of the Jordan Evans Group, a leadership consulting business. Formerly one of the consulting partners and senior vice president of the Change Management Practice at Drake Beam Morin, she now focuses on executive coaching, team building and succession planning. She holds a master's degree in organization development. Sharon (originally from the Northwest) lives in Woodland Hills and Cambria, California, with her husband Mike. Her four grown children, Shelby, Travis, Matt and Kellie, are also on the West Coast.

Beverly and Sharon can be spotted at Starbucks, on airplanes or on long exercise walks, anywhere.

While Bev and Sharon use their complementary skills to give keynote speeches and co-consult with a great variety of organizations, they also offer additional opportunities to individuals and organizations who wish to go further or deeper to meet their retention objectives.

Beverly Kaye & Associates Inc. and Career Systems International

Instruments, tools, inventories, workshops, and training of trainer programs are available to support your retention needs. Career development, coaching and mentoring seminars and interventions are also offered. Materials help the individual contributor, manager, or human resource professional who wishes to deliver more practical applications to their employee population.

Career Systems International, Inc.
900 James Avenue, Scranton, PA 18510
Office (800) 577-6916; Fax (570) 346-8606; Email HQ@csibka.com
Web site: www.careersystemsintl.com

Sharon Jordan-Evans and The Jordan Evans Group

Executive one-on-one coaching for those talented people whom you want to develop, organization development interventions designed and tailored to your specific needs. 360-degree feedback, competency development and other assessment processes designed to retain and develop skills at mid-manager and senior levels.

The Jordan Evans Group
22120 Dumetz Road, Woodland Hills, CA 91364
Office (818) 347-6565; Fax (818) 347-6577; Email Jordevans@aol.com
Web site: www.jeg.org